This bird's eye view of Sioux Falls in 1882 appeared in the December 7, 1882, issue of the Sioux Falls Pantagraph. *The two newest additions to the town are featured in the upper corners: the giant Queen Bee Mill and the Cataract House. The large building left of center is Central School, and Phillips Avenue includes larger buildings than had yet been built. The west edge of town is just beyond Summit Avenue and the south edge is Fourteenth Street. It was a practice for developers to lay out blocks and plant trees around them in anticipation of home builders who would want shade trees as soon as possible. There were no trees when the town was founded except along the river and on the small islands in the river.*

We are pleased to bring you this special Author's Edition of *Sioux Falls, South Dakota: A Pictorial History.* The first edition, sponsored by First National Bank as part of its centennial observance, was a popular success, selling the entire run of three thousand copies in less than two months. Requests from many Sioux Falls' residents, who were unable to purchase a copy of the first edition, prompted the publication of this one.

This edition has allowed us to correct some minor errors of fact and to add some pictures that were not available when we prepared the first edition. For example, when preparing the first edition, we looked diligently for a photo of President Woodrow Wilson, when he was in Sioux Falls in 1919, but we were unable to find one. After the book appeared we commented on this disappointment during a television interview and the next day Bill Kolb brought us the postcard photo found in this edition. It is the newly added photos that make this a special edition.

Two years have passed since the first edition appeared, and Sioux Falls has continued to grow and change during this time. Consequently, we have included some new photos and text to document these recent changes.

Again, we want to say thank you to those who graciously shared photos and information with us in the preparation of this book. You made this book possible.

Garry D. Olson

Erik L. Olson

December 1, 1987

Sioux Falls, South Dakota
A PICTORIAL HISTORY

by

**Gary D. Olson
and Erik L. Olson**

design by
Paula Hennigan Phillips

The Donning Company/Publishers
Norfolk/Virginia Beach

The Donning Company/Publishers
5659 Virginia Beach Boulevard
Norfolk, Virginia 23502

Edited by Richard A. Horwege

Library of Congress Cataloging-in-Publication Data

Olson, Gary D.
  Sioux Falls: a pictorial history.

  Bibliography: p.
  Includes index.
  1. Sioux Falls (S.D.)—History—Pictorial works. 2. Sioux
Falls (S.D.)—Description—Views. I. Olson, Erik L. II. Title.
F659.S6047   1985   978.3'371   85-20611
ISBN 0-89865-436-X

Printed in the United States of America

Table of Contents

SIOUX FALLS S.D.

BEST IN THE WEST

Foreword

A leader of a tribe of the Northern Plains once observed that "A people without history is like wind on the buffalo grass." History is more than a chronicle of great events and times long-past; it is as mundane as two farmers standing in their corn, one thousand years ago, worrying about the rain, and it is as near as yesterday. What happens in our home, or our neighborhood, or our town, has more impact on our lives than most events played out on the national stage. Change is the only constant, sometimes dramatic, sometimes almost imperceptible. As peoples and cultures grow and adapt, the townscape alters as well. Our communities reflect our values and hopes, just as we are shaped by the environment in which we live. An historian's sources are many—documents, newspapers, photographs, objects, living people who recall past events and ways of life. Making sense out of such disparate material is the historian's greatest challenge. In sorting through these fragmentary survivals, a historian places past life into perspective—and the very best provide as well a vantage point for the future. No one is better suited to furnish these perspectives for Sioux Falls, than the team of Gary and Erik Olson.

Geoffrey R. Hunt
Director
Siouxland Heritage Museums

Preface

It is both exciting and sobering to present to the community this new account of its historical development. Like many other residents, we are not natives of Sioux Falls, but we have come to regard it as our home. We have learned the history of Sioux Falls through its photographic record, and thus we are delighted to be able to share this history with others. We hope that you will enjoy reading this book as much as we enjoyed writing it, and that you learn to understand Sioux Falls better through its text and pictures.

The intent of this book is not to tell a detailed history of Sioux Falls in the traditional manner of the earlier histories by Dana Bailey (1899), Charles Smith (1949), and Reuben Bragstad (1967). This is, instead, an interpretive and visual history. The brief text that introduces each chapter seeks to identify the major developments in Sioux Falls during each time period and to interpret why and how they occurred. Except where we have directly quoted an author's words, we have generally not footnoted the sources of our factual information. This book is intended for a general audience and thus the extensive scholarly apparatus of formal academic works has not been included. We have drawn our information from the large number of sources that are listed in the bibliography at the end of the volume. Some readers will wonder why we neglected to mention some event or topic in the chapter introductions, but as you proceed beyond the introductory text of each chapter we think you will find most of the topics addressed in the photo captions. Still, much has of necessity been left out to keep the book to a manageable size. The photographs are the real strength of this book, for they convey the changes our city has experienced better than our words could ever do.

Authors nearly always incur debts of gratitude for the assistance given by others in making their book possible. Certainly this is true for us, and we would be remiss if we did not express our deep appreciation to all those who have helped us. We hope you who assisted us will feel that this is in part your book, and that you take pride in your contribution.

Our first thanks must, of course, go to the First National Bank of Sioux Falls for sponsoring this publication. Founded in 1885, First National Bank (Minnehaha National Bank, prior to 1929) has been part of the history of Sioux Falls for one hundred years. Sponsoring a new history of the city is a centennial commemoration of lasting value to the community.

We are also indebted to those who have provided us access to the photographs that are the heart of this book. We are fortunate to have two major photographic repositories in the community—the Siouxland Heritage Museums and the Center for Western Studies—and both graciously allowed us access to their collections. Special thanks go to Harry Thompson, archivist at the Center for Western Studies, and to Geoffrey Hunt, Director of the Siouxland Heritage Museums for their cordial cooperation and help. It is ironic but true that good photographs of Sioux Falls are more difficult to find for the modern, more recent period than for earlier ones. For this reason we are especially indebted to two people, to Richard Munce for sharing his snapshots of downtown Sioux Falls in the 1940s and early 1950s, and to Joel Strasser for allowing us to use some of his splendid photos of the city for the period since 1950. We also thank all those who read about our project and called to offer pictures and all those we called in search of pictures and information. We have credited all whose pictures we used, but we also thank those who loaned us pictures we ended up having to leave out. We encourage all who have photos of this city to give them to the Center for Western Studies or the Siouxland Heritage Museums or at least allow them to copy them and add them to their photo archives. Photos are fragile records of our history and need to be preserved for the future.

A final and very special word of appreciation must go to Rosaaen Olson who tolerated the pictures and notes that cluttered our home during the project, turned the kitchen table into a work station, and typed our manuscript. She typed it that hard, old-fashioned way—with a typewriter—that required two full versions of the text. Her typing skills, cheerful support and patience made this a successful family project.

Gary D. Olson

Erik L. Olson

This photo from the early 1870s shows the
falls as they looked in 1856 when the men
of the Western Town Company and rival
Dakota Land Company arrived to claim
the land. Both parties thought the power of
the falls would make the area a valuable
townsite. It was said that these falls could
be heard from a distance of three miles.
Note the absence of trees. Center for
Western Studies photo

In the Beginning

Unlike some places where towns have grown from the soil of the midwestern prairie, this place is defined by a special geographical feature—the falls of the Big Sioux River. The river valley was formed in the last great ice age as melted ice channeled its way through the soil and rock released by the glacier and flowed downward along the glacier's receding edge. At this place the river's course dropped over the bedrock quartzite nearly one hundred feet in less than half a mile. Other natural attributes, too, made this a special place long before white men came to build a town. A mineral spring with healing qualities flowed from the hillside west of the falls, and the high bluffs provided ancient peoples village sites that could be easily defended.

We know of the early inhabitants of this place from the visible burial mounds they built and from the village sites that have been uncovered. Archeologists, who have examined the mounds and village sites, tell us that these mound builders were a hunting people who inhabited this area in the period from roughly A.D. 500 to 800. In the centuries after A.D. 800 a different, agricultural people moved into the area. Identified by anthropologists as the ancestors of the historic Mandan Indians, these people established fortified villages at many of the sites that had attracted the mound builders. There are a large number of mounds along the Big Sioux River and village sites near Brandon and Blood Run as well as at Sherman Park. In the eighteenth century the Lakota Indians moved into this area, driven westward by their eastern enemies who had obtained firearms from the whites. When they arrived at this place the mounds and village sites of their predecessors were already

The Sherman Park Indian Mounds were the burial grounds for Indians that lived in eastern South Dakota twelve hundred to sixteen hundred years ago. When the first white settlers arrived in the area in the middle of the nineteenth century the mounds were objects of curiosity. According to records, some of the troopers at Fort Dakota between 1865 and 1869 dug into the mounds at Sherman Park, and in 1873 R. F. Pettigrew and his brother Fred also sought to satisfy their curiosity with pick and shovel. The Pettigrew brothers exhumed some pottery and stone implements which formed the original basis of the Indian collection given to the city by Senator Pettigrew upon his death in 1926.

More recently, in 1962, an archeological team from the University of South Dakota excavated one of the five burial mounds located on the crest of the hill in Sherman Park. Through careful removal of the earth, one shallow layer at a time with mason's trowel and brush and screening all the loose dirt, the archeologists recovered everything in the mound down to bits of wood, bone, and pottery. From their findings it is clear that later inhabitants of the area had used these ancient mounds for their own purposes. A wooden coffin with iron nails and the skeleton of a buffalo were found near the top of the mound as were the bones of a horse that had been shot with a bullet. Lower in the mound the remains of five human skeletons were discovered together with rings, copper, and shell beads. These were presumably placed in the mound by the people who originally constructed the earthen tomb. These mounds remind us that this area is much older than the history of its Anglo-American inhabitants. Center for Western Studies photo

centuries old. The Indian mounds remind us that white men are only the most recent people to make their homes by the falls of the Big Sioux.

The earliest Europeans to visit the falls of the Big Sioux were undoubtedly French explorers and fur traders. The area was part of the French colonial area called Louisiana until it was ceded to Spain in 1763 following the French and Indian War. Although the French, operating from bases on the Mississippi River and Great Lakes, had difficulty carrying on a trade with the Sioux (they were too closely allied to Sioux enemies to the east), it seems clear from a French map of 1701 that Sioux Falls was a rendezvous for Indians and French fur traders. After ownership of Louisiana was transferred to Spain, British fur companies dominated the trade in the area through French *coureurs de bois* who continued their activities from bases in Canada or on the Mississippi. Spain tried hard to counter these British incursions into its territory but

made little progress prior to the transfer of Louisiana back to France in 1801.

In 1804 the Sioux Falls area came under the jurisdiction of the United States when President Thomas Jefferson purchased Louisiana from Napoleon Bonaparte. Operating out of St. Louis, American fur traders sought to win the tribes of the upper Missouri away from their well-established British rivals. British traders had developed good relations with the tribes of this area, and not until after the War of 1812 did American influence in the area increase significantly.

Beginning with the Lewis and Clark Expedition in 1804-1806, numerous government and private exploring parties travelled up the Missouri River. It has been asserted that the earliest explorer to visit the falls of the Big Sioux was Joseph Nicolas Nicollet, a distinguished French scientist, hired by the United States government in 1838 to explore and map the region between the upper Mississippi and Missouri

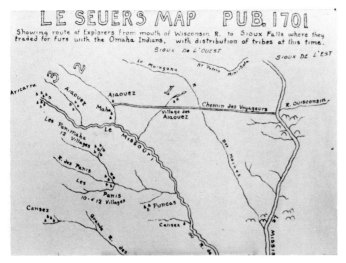

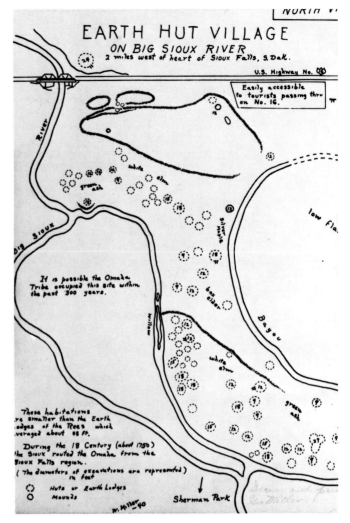

This map, published in Paris in 1701, shows a fur trader's trail from the falls of the Big Sioux River to Prairie du Chien on the Mississippi. The Iowa and Omaha tribes lived in this area at that time. Center for Western Studies photo

An early Indian village site in the area of present day Sherman Park is shown on this map. Indians lived in and travelled through the area hundreds of years before the white man came. George Miller map, 1940, Siouxland Heritage Museums

rivers. Indeed, old accounts credit Nicollet's report of his explorations, published in 1839, with initiating interest in the falls as a potential townsite among speculators in Dubuque, Iowa, in the mid-1850s. But a careful reading of Nicollet's report reveals that he explored westward through Minnesota to the pipestone quarry and then moved northward to Lake Kampeska before turning eastward to the Minnesota River. He never visited the falls of the Big Sioux. It seems more likely that the report of the falls that set the Dubuque speculators in motion was that of Capt. Joseph Allen who, with a detachment of soldiers, camped at the falls on September 13, 1844, while exploring the Big Sioux River.

Until 1851 this area was part of the hunting grounds claimed by the Santee Lakota. In that year the Santee signed the Treaty of Traverse des Sioux in which they ceded title to all their land east of the Big Sioux River except for a reservation along the western part of the Minnesota River. Technically this allowed townsite speculators from Iowa and Minnesota to establish a claim to land around the falls as long as they stayed on the east side of the Big Sioux. In 1858 the Yankton Lakota Tribe signed a treaty ceding to the United States government all its land between the Sioux and Missouri rivers. Only at this point could settlers stake their claim to land on the west side of the Big Sioux River.

It took several years before all the bands of the Yankton Lakota recognized the treaty that gave the falls of the Big Sioux to the white man. Indeed, a military post was needed for a brief time to provide security against Indian attacks. By 1869 the Indian threat in the area was past. Indian bands continued to visit Sioux Falls regularly for the next decade or so, but it was to visit the mineral spring or to stop over on their way to or from the pipestone quarry. The federal census taker in June of 1880 noted that a band of forty Indians was camped just outside of town.

The original Sioux Falls Brewery and Malting Works is shown here in the late 1870s on north Main Avenue. In 1904 the buildings west of Main Avenue were replaced by the tall, stone, castle-like building still standing. Center for Western Studies photo

The Founding Period
1856 to 1878

The founding of Sioux Falls is part of the frontier history of this nation, and the process of its founding was driven by the same forces that created countless other towns across the continent. The American frontier in the mid-nineteenth century was the land of opportunity, and many men and some women made their fortunes on the western frontier. New England and western Europe were crowded with people who longed for land and had none or too little, while the American West consisted of vast expanses of fertile, virgin land and few people. It was the land that could make people rich. But ironically great wealth did not come from plowing and planting the land. It came from selling it.

Land speculation was the mania of nineteenth-century America. The way to make easy money was to buy land cheap (or to get it for nothing) and sell it at a higher price. Money could be made by selling farm land, but far greater opportunities for wealth existed in townsite development. Farm land was bought and sold by the acre, but townsites were bought by the acre and sold by the town block and lot. The profit margin could be greater on commercial property, but only if people came who wanted to buy it. Townsite speculators thus of necessity became promoters of frontier settlement.

It was the possibility of making great wealth through the founding of towns that was the key to the rapid settlement of the American frontier. Men rushed to be the first to acquire the most likely townsites on the frontier. They sought out those sites that possessed natural assets for becoming a town and perhaps even a city. A railroad could create a successful town even if the location lacked natural assets, but before railroads

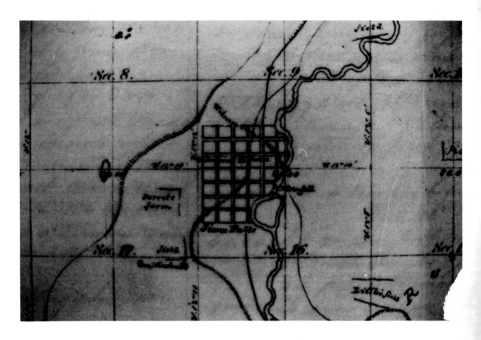

The United States government survey of Sioux Falls in 1859 shows how the townsite was laid out prior to its abandonment in 1862. Present day Fifth Street was the southern boundary of the settlement. In 1870, after Fort Dakota was abandoned, J. L. Phillips laid out downtown Sioux Falls where it is today based on the location of the fort buildings rather than at the earlier site. Center for Western Studies photo

the most promising townsites were by rivers. A navigable river allowed a town to become a river port and prosper from riverboat commerce. Rivers too small for navigation could provide a successful townsite if the power of its current could be harnessed. Water power, either from natural falls or man-made dams, could drive mills and factories and virtually guarantee the development of a successful town or city.

It was the falls of the Big Sioux River that made this location a prime townsite, and in 1856 two groups of speculators, one in St. Paul, Minnesota, and a second in Dubuque, Iowa, organized for the purpose of claiming the land around the falls. In that year a feverish epidemic of speculation swept across Iowa and Minnesota, and legislators did little else than charter railroad and townsite companies. The idea was to claim the best townsites, have railroads built to them and make them the county seats as the territory filled with settlers. Real estate would bring premium prices at townsites having some natural assets, a railroad connection to the outside world and the county courthouse. The St. Paul group, incorporated as the Dakota Land Company, had even bigger aspirations for the Sioux Falls townsite. Their strategy was to have Minnesota become a state (1858) with the falls of the Big Sioux River left outside its western boundary. They were confident that their connections with the Democratic administration of Pres. James Buchanan would result in Sioux Falls being designated a capital of the new territory of Dakota.

From the outset the Dakota Land Company's ambitious plans were frustrated. They came to the falls of the Big Sioux in the spring of 1857 only to discover they were too late. The Dubuque-based Western Town Company had arrived a few days earlier and claimed the main townsite, the 320 acres

adjacent to the falls. The Minnesota group had to b content with a 320-acre claim well above the falls which they christened Sioux Falls City. Nor did their expectations that the Buchanan administration would establish Dakota Territory and designate Sioux Falls as its capital materialize. The sectional rancour that ultimately resulted in the Civil War prevented the Democrats from giving Dakota territorial status until 1861 and in that year the Republican party acquired the presidency and control of Congress. President Buchanan signed the Dakota Territorial Act on March 2, two days before leaving office. Consequently, the Republican administration of Abraham Lincoln appointed territorial officials and designated Yankton the territorial capital.

The two companies claimed the land around the falls under the Preemption Act of 1841. Under this act they could buy the land for $1.25 an acre after building a house, cultivating a minimum of five acres and living on the land a minimum of six months. They quickly laid out streets, blocks and building lots. The normal city block contains about two and one-half acres. If one ignores the cost of land that became streets, these founders of Sioux Falls paid $3.15 per city block and anticipated selling building lots for a minimum of $50.00 and premium commercial lots for $200.00 or more.

Unfortunately, their dream did not materialize so easily. In 1857 an economic depression again engulfed the nation, and the stream of settlers rushing to take up land on the frontier slowed to a trickle. Nor did plans for building railroads across Iowa and Minnesota materialize. Even worse, Indians threatened the settlement in 1858, but the representatives of the two land companies allied to build a fort from sod and defend their settlement. Consequently, the settlement failed

Fort Dakota is shown here on the site of Sioux Falls in 1866. The earlier Sioux Falls settlement had been abandoned in 1862 because of the Indian scare and sat empty until the fort was established in 1865. Established after the Civil War to protect settlers from Indian attacks, Fort Dakota existed until the spring of 1869. Siouxland Heritage Museums photo

to grow much larger than thirty to forty residents, most of whom were members of the two land companies waiting for the return of good times and the arrival of a fresh stream of settlers.

But conditions failed to improve. In 1861 the nation's attention and energies became focused on the Civil War and troops were rushed from the frontier to the battle fronts in the East and South. In Minnesota the Santee Sioux seized this opportunity to rebel against the treatment they had suffered on their reservation along the Minnesota River. In August of 1862 the Santee launched a murderous attack upon settlers in southwestern Minnesota, and before the end of the month the Indian uprising reached Sioux Falls.

Sioux Falls was not unprotected. A detachment of volunteer cavalry, organized by Gov. William Jayne in the winter of 1861-62, was stationed at the settlement. The attack, however, came without noise and fanfare. On August 25, 1862, Judge J. B. Amidon and his son failed to return after a day of gathering hay on their field on the bluff overlooking the river. Searchers found them the next morning, dead from gunshot and arrow wounds, and soon after a band of Indians was sighted. But the Indians did not attack. The presence of the cavalry apparently discouraged them.

A few days later the settlement received news of the Indian massacres in Minnesota, and the governor ordered the cavalry unit to escort the settlers to the safety of Yankton. The townsite was abandoned to the ravages of the Indians and prairie fires. Abandoned, too, were the immediate hopes of the townsite speculators for making their fortunes at Sioux Falls. Two years later visitors to the abandoned settlement found most of the buildings burned and streets and trails overgrown with grass and brush.

The townsite promoters sought to revive their plans for Sioux Falls by persuading the federal government to establish a military post in the area. An army fort would provide the sense of security needed to encourage settlers to return to the Big Sioux River Valley. Petitions from the territorial legislature received no response until the Civil War had been concluded. But in the spring of 1865 Company E of the Sixth Iowa Cavalry established Fort Dakota just above the main falls and marked off a military reservation measuring seven by ten miles surrounding it.

The fort did bring a sense of security to the area, and the end of the Civil War revived the flow of settlers to the Big Sioux Valley. In 1866 Norwegian settlers arrived to claim land in the valley north of the military reservation and more followed in succeeding months. But the presence of Fort Dakota, while stimulating settlement, also frustrated the ambitions of the men who wished to reestablish their claims to the townsite around the falls. No civilians were allowed to claim land or settle on a military reservation. Consequently, almost from the moment Fort Dakota was established, the men who had worked so hard to convince the government to establish it began working to convince the government to abandon it. The government responded to their petitions by withdrawing troops from the fort in June of 1869.

Several of the original townsite claimants watched the soldiers leave Fort Dakota on June 18, but were unable to reestablish their claims. Government policy for disposing of military reservations required that the land be auctioned off in Washington, D.C., to the highest bidder. This was a prime townsite and the land would bring high prices at auction. It was sure to be grabbed up by wealthy speculator-investors in the East.

The commander of Fort Dakota is entertaining visitors in this 1866 photo of the officers' quarters. J. L. Phillips and his family used the officers' quarters at Fort Dakota as their first home when they came to Sioux Falls in 1870. Center for Western Studies photo

This is the stone Commissary at Fort Dakota. The fort was located between Seventh and Ninth near Phillips Avenue. A plaque on the Hollywood Theatre marks the vicinity of its location. Center for Western Studies photo

Richard F. Pettigrew had this painting commissioned to show what Sioux Falls looked like when he first came in 1869. All that existed were the fort buildings and Seney Island, which can be seen directly above the falls. Note the fortified stone tower to the right of the barracks, the stables at the river's edge, the post hospital on the extreme left, and the Yankton Trail crossing the river at what came to be Ninth Street. Siouxland Heritage Museums photo

After the army abandoned Fort Dakota in 1870, the buildings were used by the settlers who were allowed to live on the reservation site for the first time. This is the west side of Phillips Avenue, north of Eighth Street about 1872-73. The old barracks building was used as a store, post office, and school before being removed in July 1873. Center for Western Studies photo

But fortune smiled on the men from Dubuque and St. Paul whose prospects seemed so bleak. Late in June a government surveying party stopped at the falls before heading out on the Dakota prairie for a summer of survey work. Richard F. Pettigrew, a college student, and a member of this surveying party, possessed the connections necessary to help the local townsite hopefuls. Pettigrew's classmate at the University of Wisconsin was the brother of Sen. Matthew Carpenter. Through this connection Pettigrew was able to get a special bill passed in Congress allowing the Fort Dakota Reservation to be disposed of under the normal federal land laws, i.e., preemption and homesteading. This allowed the Dubuque and St. Paul men to file their claims to the land around the falls and the young Pettigrew was cut in on a piece of the action. When he came back in the spring of 1870 Pettigrew traded his college career for one in real estate. He quickly became a leading promoter of Sioux Falls, a wealthy man, and a successful politician.

The original land companies had long since dissolved, but several of the participants laid claim under the Preemption Act to land that today is Sioux Falls. Dr. J. L. Phillips, formerly of the Western Town Company, laid claim to the quarter section that included Fort Dakota and present day downtown Sioux Falls. When the fort buildings were auctioned off in the summer of 1870 Phillips bought them for next to nothing for no one bid against him.

The second Sioux Falls, which began in 1870, evolved from the existing buildings of Fort Dakota. In November, Charlie (C. K.) Howard, a merchant from Sioux City, built a frame addition to the fort hospital at about 10th Street and Phillips Avenue and opened a store. Pettigrew and a few others lived in the old barracks and Dr. Phillips moved his family into the fort officers' quarters. During the winter of 1870-71 Phillips laid out streets and lots from Sixth to Ninth streets and between Phillips and Minnesota avenues.

None of the fort buildings were located exactly on the grid of streets and blocks that Phillips established, and consequently, as new buildings were constructed the fort structures were one by one abandoned and razed. Pettigrew began the building activity in April of 1871 by erecting a small office on the west side of Phillips Avenue, a little north of Eighth Street. Later that spring Harry Corson and his family arrived in a covered wagon and after buying a lot from Phillips at the corner of Ninth and Phillips began constructing the Cataract Hotel. During the summer a second hotel, the Central House, and the Van Eps Store were added to the new settlement. Construction of more store buildings and houses continued in 1872 and 1873. In July of 1873 the last fort building, one of the barracks, was demolished.

It was, of course, crucial that Sioux Falls retain its status as county seat, but in 1872 Dell Rapids emerged as a possible rival for the distinction. Dell Rapids was more centrally located in the Minnehaha County that also included present-day Moody County. Again, it was Pettigrew who saved the day. He had been elected to the 1872 legislature but had not been allowed to take his seat due to some elections irregularities. He remained in Yankton, however, and

This photo looks north on Phillips Avenue from Eleventh Street in about 1876. Sidewalks were not required until 1877. The United States Land Office is at left and C. K. Howard's General Store is next to it. E. A. Sherman erected the first brick building, just left of Center, in 1875. Center for Western Studies photo

maneuvered behind the scenes when the legislature established county boundaries. He arranged for the creation of Moody County so as to put its southern border so close to Dell Rapids that it lost its central location in Minnehaha County. As an additional benefit, the boundary just happened to make Pettigrew's brother's homestead a central location in the new Moody County, and he laid out the town of Flandreau on it as the county seat.

Securely in possession of their claims to the townsite, Phillips, Pettigrew and the others turned their energies to attracting settlers to their new town. While many promotional activities were launched to encourage people to move to Sioux Falls from Wisconsin, eastern Iowa and places even further east, these founders of Sioux Falls clearly understood that the key to real growth and prosperity for their townsite was the acquisition of a railroad connection to the outside world. Efforts to gain a railroad began in 1873 when a rail line was completed from Minneapolis, through Worthington, to Sioux City, but in that year the worst economic depression in the nation's history, aside from that of the 1930s, brought hopes of an early rail connection to a sudden halt. The frontier needed credit to develop farms, businesses and railroads, and with the onset of the depression no credit was available.

The year 1873 had been one of exciting growth for Sioux Falls. The United States Land Office was opened in Sioux Falls and did a steady business that summer and fall as settlers flocked to take up home-

steads in the surrounding countryside. Several new businesses were opened along Phillips Avenue, churches were built and the school district organized. By the end of the year the population totalled 593 residents.

But the depression and the coming of the grasshoppers put further growth plans on hold. Rocky Mountain locusts had visited some areas in 1873, but it was in 1874 that their impact was felt in the Big Sioux Valley. They came on a northwest wind late in July, just as the wheat crop was ripening, and with ravenous appetites devoured the settler's expectations of a good harvest that would enable them to pay off loans and purchase supplies for the winter. Despite relief efforts by local businessmen and eventually by the government, many settlers were forced to give up their claims and return to the East. Few new settlers arrived to take their places. Both the depression and the grasshoppers persisted for the next several years, and as a result, the population of Sioux Falls remained static until 1878.

The founders of Sioux Falls had their expectations of quick and easy wealth through the establishment of a townsite at the falls of the Big Sioux frustrated at nearly every turn. First it was the Indians and then it was depression and grasshoppers. Would success ever come? Pettigrew, Phillips, Howard, Corson and the other founders stuck it out through the hard times of the mid-seventies. These optimists were sure that good times would return and that they and their townsite would prosper together.

This early newspaper advertisement is for C. K. Howard's General Store. His generosity with credit during the hard times of the mid-1870s kept many early settlers from giving up and leaving the area. Many stories about Charlie Howard have survived. One is about a settler coming in with a cow to settle his account with Howard in the bleak grasshopper years of the seventies. As they visited, Howard learned that this was the man's only cow, and that he had a large family at home. Charlie cussed the man up one side and down the other for leaving his family without a source of milk and sent him home with two cows. Charlie Howard had a big heart, but he also realized that if settlers left the area he would have no customers at all when times got better. Sioux Falls Pantagraph, October 23, 1878

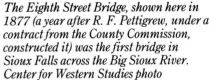

The Eighth Street Bridge, shown here in 1877 (a year after R. F. Pettigrew, under a contract from the County Commission, constructed it) was the first bridge in Sioux Falls across the Big Sioux River. Center for Western Studies photo

This west side view of Phillips Avenue from Ninth Street is looking north in about 1877. Center for Western Studies photo

15

Although there was no longer an Indian scare in Sioux Falls after 1870, bands of Indians continued to live near and visit the town for several years. This picture was reportedly taken outside of Sioux Falls in 1872. Raleigh Nelson photo

William Van Eps (1842-1906), born in Wisconsin, came to Sioux Falls from Cherokee, Iowa, for the first time in August 1870, and as he put it, "became infatuated with the country." His first store, which he built in the spring of 1871, was a combination store and home, as he and his wife lived upstairs. Van Eps was a leading Democrat in a predominately Republican city and state. His large Victorian home stood on the site of the current bus depot and Van Eps Park. Photo from Dana Bailey's History of Minnehaha County

The William Van Eps Store, located at Eighth and Phillips, was photographed in about 1877. By this time the city had grown to nearly six hundred people. Van Eps built the store in 1871, when the first buildings were erected along Phillips Avenue, and he continued to be one of the leading merchants of the growing community for the next several decades. Center for Western Studies photo

The first Cataract Hotel was built in 1871 by Harry Corson at Ninth and Phillips. The Cataract was the place to stay and eat in early Sioux Falls. As the place where all important local meetings occurred, the Cataract was regarded as the center of the city. Consequently, in 1886 when a system of house numbering was first established, it began at the intersection of Ninth and Phillips. Center for Western Studies photo

This photo looks northeast from about Tenth and Main in about 1875. Sioux Falls was still a one-street town along Phillips Avenue between Seventh and Tenth streets. Center for Western Studies photo

Harry Corson, was the founder of the Cataract Hotel in 1871. In 1877 a visitor in Sioux Falls described his stay at the Cataract Hotel in a letter to the editor of the Pantagraph *(December 5, 1877). Harry Corson, he wrote, "keeps the boss hotel of the Northwest—fried oysters for breakfast cooked to a turn—soup and turkey ditto, and a variety of other meats, poultry and dessert." Photo from Dana Bailey's,* History of Minnehaha County

This stage lines ad is from the October 23, 1878, Sioux Falls Pantagraph. *Stage lines were the equivalent of today's bus companies. They provided scheduled travel from Sioux Falls to neighboring towns before the building of the faster, safer, and more comfortable railroads.*

Seney Island, just south of the falls, was a popular picnic area for early settlers. In 1907 the Sioux Falls Light and Power Company raised the mill dam by closing the channel around the island. The Milwaukee Railroad later bought the land to expand its freight yards. Center for Western Studies photo

Richard F. (Frank) Pettigrew came to Sioux Falls in 1869 as a surveyor. Largely through his connections in Washington, D.C., the Fort Dakota military reservation land was opened to local individuals, including himself, under the Preemption and Homestead acts. Center for Western Studies photo

The Galesburg Addition was named for Artemus Gale, an original member of the Dakota Land Company who claimed this area in 1870 when the Fort Dakota reservation was open to settlers. This late 1870s view of Galesburg shows the area south of Twelfth and east of Phillips Avenue. Center for Western Studies photo

Artemas Gale, born in New Jersey in 1825, was a successful realtor and merchant in St. Paul before coming to Sioux Falls in 1870. He claimed four hundred acres of land using half-breed script, and on this land he platted the Galesburg Addition where he built his home. He remained in Sioux Falls for the remainder of his life. Photo from Dana Bailey's History of Minnehaha County

C. K. (Charlie) Howard, a Sioux City merchant, first came to Sioux Falls in about 1867 and operated the Sutler's Store at Fort Dakota, trading with the soldiers as well as Indians and settlers in the area. Upon abandonment of the fort in 1870 he purchased the old hospital, moved to Sioux Falls and opened his store in the new town. In 1872 he built a new store building on the corner of Tenth and Phillips. Howard helped many settlers survive the depression and grasshopper plagues of the mid-1870s by extending generous credit. He prospered after 1877 and sold out in 1884 to take up ranching southwest of the city and later in the Black Hills. He gave five thousand dollars to help establish the School for the Deaf in Sioux Falls. His generosity combined with some poor investments resulted in bankruptcy toward the end of his career. He died penniless in 1918. Sioux Falls citizens raised five thousand dollars to bury and provide a suitable cemetery marker for Charlie Howard. Center for Western Studies photo

The first train that steamed into Sioux Falls on July 30, 1878, looked much like this St. Paul and Pacific (a division of the Great Northern) engine. A railroad helped to guarantee that Sioux Falls would survive and probably prosper as a city. Eventually Sioux Falls was served by seven railroads. Center for Western Studies photo

Boom and Bust
1878 to 1898

In 1878 good times returned and the grasshoppers did not. The nation had worked its way out of the severe depression that began in 1873, and both investors and speculators regained the sense of optimism that rapid economic growth requires. Railroads in Minnesota and Iowa reorganized and launched vigorous campaigns to tap the potential markets of Dakota. The result was the Dakota Boom. The new wave of homesteaders began in 1878, crested in 1884, and gradually receded thereafter until the Panic of 1893 and the depression that followed again brought it to a virtual halt. Between 1880 and 1885, the total amount of land claimed under preemption, homestead, and timber culture laws in Dakota far exceeded any other state or territory in the nation. When South Dakota became a state in 1889 the Dakota Boom was over. By then the land east of the Missouri River was settled, and the onset of the Depression of 1893 resulted in a net decrease in population by the end of the nineties.

Sioux Falls shared fully in the boom-and-bust cycle of the last two decades of the century. The city experienced a sustained period of exciting growth between 1878 and 1890. Its downtown was transformed from a single street (Phillips Avenue) of one and two story frame buildings with false fronts to an impressive business district stretching from the river to Minnesota Avenue and from Twelfth to Sixth streets. Frame structures were replaced by larger, multi-storied brick and stone buildings, and new government buildings, churches and schools created a city skyline. And industry came too. It began with the power of the falls, but industry quickly turned to more dependable steam power and was freed to locate

away from the river.

What caused the city's impressive growth and development in the 1880s? Was it the water power of the falls? No. Despite the early confidence that this natural asset would be the basis of the city's success, the falls never contributed in any substantial way to the city's growth. It was its location and transportation that made Sioux Falls grow. Located far enough away from Sioux City and St. Paul, it became a distributing center for the region around it and westward into the state. But other townsites near Sioux Falls could have gained the same advantage. Why did Sioux Falls become the regional transportation and distributing center? A writer in 1885 was probably right when he declared it was due to its "old timers—the men of indomitable pluck, energy, enterprise and generous impulses...." (City Directory, 1885, p. 14) Men like J. L. Phillips, R. F. Pettigrew, E. A. Sherman, P. P. Peck, S. L. Tate, and L. T. Dunning and others out-promoted rival townsites. In doing so they built a city and their personal fortunes at the same time.

Sioux Falls promoters, like those of any nineteenth-century frontier townsite, recognized that the key to their success would be transportation. Only a railroad, not the plodding transit of oxen or horses and wagons, could move bulky agricultural produce, manufactured goods and people quickly, cheaply and dependably.

Yankton had secured a rail connection in February 1873, just ahead of the depression that smashed the early railroad hopes of Sioux Falls promoters. Consequently, Sioux Falls was in a hurry to catch up. Young Richard F. Pettigrew led the efforts to secure a railroad during the mid-1870s largely because he had the means and time needed to lobby the railroad companies and visit potential investors. While others suffered from the depression and grasshoppers, Pettigrew managed to secure surveying contracts from the federal government each summer that provided him a steady income. He travelled to St. Paul regularly between 1873 and 1876 to convince the railroad men to build the sixty-five mile branch from Worthington to Sioux Falls. In 1876 the St. Paul and Sioux City Railroad Company finally agreed to build the line if Sioux Falls would furnish a thirty-five thousand dollar cash bonus and fifteen thousand dollars more in right-of-way and depot grounds. It was a high price, but the future of the town was at stake and the proposition was accepted.

On July 30, 1878, the first train steamed into Sioux Falls. The *Sioux Falls Pantagraph* reported the next day, "we are all wonderfully glad...that the iron horse has got here, because it is what Sioux Falls has been looking forward to for a long, long time." Sioux Falls was now a railhead; a place where new settlers disembarked and outfitted before heading out onto the prairie to take up a homestead; a place where retail prices were cheaper because transportation costs were less; and where settlers came to sell their crops and purchase supplies.

The impact of the rail connection was immediate and dramatic. The population jumped from 600 to 2,164 in less than three years and buildings were erected at a feverish rate. But Sioux Falls promoters were not content with only one railroad. They were determined to make Sioux Falls a rail center, and to a large extent they succeeded. Although it never ac-

Central School, built in 1878 at the present site of Washington High School, was the first brick school building in Sioux Falls. With the coming of the railroad, the school was soon overcrowded and five additional schools were built in the next fourteen years. Central was razed in 1935 to make room for the west wing of Washington High. Siouxland Heritage Museum photo

quired a mainline connection, Sioux Falls did receive a total of five rail connections to the east by 1888. In each case the city gave depot grounds and right-of-way to the railroad. Just as important to its growth, Sioux Falls also extended rail lines westward that made it the regional distributing and marketing center. As a result, the city's population continued to grow by an average of over 1,000 people per year throughout the 1880s, totalling 10,167 by 1890. If farm prices had been better during these years, Sioux Falls' growth and prosperity would have been even greater.

As a rapidly growing community, Sioux Falls had to address many important civic issues after 1878. Residents demanded public improvements and services such as better streets, schools, fire protection and water supplies. The key to solving these needs was the establishment of an effective form of local government. Prior to 1877 the town was under the jurisdiction of the Minnehaha County Commission which paid little attention to its needs. Thus, the incorporation of Sioux Falls as a self-governing village by the territorial legislature in 1876 was an important event. The first resolution of the Village Board of Trustees in 1877 was to require sidewalks on Phillips Avenue. The rapid growth of the community after 1878 soon required a governmental structure that provided more latitude of action, and in 1883 the legislature granted Sioux Falls a city charter. The new charter authorized a mayor and council form of city government with two aldermen representing each ward.

The new city government addressed the pressing needs of the community with uneven results. A volunteer fire department had been organized in 1877 and a steam fire engine purchased in 1881, but not until 1884 was a more organized system of fire protection established. In that same year the city gave a franchise to the South Dakota Water Company, a private corporation based in Pittsburg, Pennsylvania, to provide a water system for the city. It took water from the river at Eighth Street and pumped it through underground pipes to homes and businesses. Complaints about the quality of the water grew louder as pollution of the river increased, but not until 1907 did the current municipal water system begin operating from a well field north of town. A major interest of the city council in the 1880s was the grading of streets and the creation of a sewage system. But although studies were done and plans drawn by outside consultants, no public sewage system was built until 1892. In 1885 the city council approved the installation of the first electric street lights and the next year gas lights were also approved. The two competing lighting systems expanded with the city until 1906 when the gas company ceased to provide street lighting. Drainage and street grades were continuing concerns in the 1880s, but no streets were paved until 1888 when Phillips Avenue was surfaced with quartzite paving stones from Fifth Street to Twelfth Street.

A public improvement of particular note is Richard F. Pettigrew's street railroad which began operations in 1887. The community had expanded so far from the downtown that it was increasingly difficult for people to get to work if they did not own a horse and carriage. A street railroad was also a public indication that Sioux Falls was a growing, prospering community, and its presence would encourage people to settle or invest in the city. Pettigrew was a city promoter, but he knew how to promote his own

25

This ad in the January 29, 1879, Panta-graph *illustrates the city's hopes that water power would make the city a manufacturing center.*

In 1879 a major effort to harness the power of the falls was made with the construction of the Queen Bee Mill. R. F. Pettigrew convinced George Seney, an eastern investor, to finance the construction of this huge, seven-story, twelve-hundred-barrel-per-day flour mill. This may be Seney posing in front of the Queen Bee during construction. Center for Western Studies photo

interests at the same time by building street car lines through his residential development areas. Lots sold easier and brought higher prices if they were along the street car line. By 1891 the system had eight miles of track.

The main preoccupation of city promoters in the 1880s was the development of local industries. Sioux Falls was not to be merely a marketing and retailing center. These men envisioned it becoming a "second Chicago." Railroads were one part of this vision, but they were a means to a larger end. Railroads would make local manufacturing feasible, and manufacturing would attract workers and workers would need houses and expand the entire community.

The industrial visions of local promoters were grandiose from the outset. In the fall of 1878 Pettigrew watched as area farmers in a "string of lumber wagons that reached clear beyond the river south of the Yankton crossing," waited to unload their wheat crop at the Sioux Falls railroad terminal. Why, he asked himself, should this wheat be shipped to Minnesota or Wisconsin to be ground into flour when Sioux Falls had the water power to do it? After interesting a St. Paul mill operator in building a mill in Sioux Falls and acquiring the land for the mill site, Pettigrew went to New York to find investors to finance the project. Pettigrew convinced George I. Seney, an investment capitalist, to come to Sioux Falls in June of 1879 to see the site and hear more about the proposed mill. To ensure that Seney was impressed by the Big Sioux's power, Pettigrew had a temporary earthen dam built across the river north of the city. Just before Seney arrived the dam was removed and the roaring power of the falls impressed the New Yorker sufficiently for him to invest his money in making Pettigrew's dream a reality. Construction on the giant mill began in August of 1879 and was completed in 1881. But after only two years of operation it closed in bankruptcy not to open again until 1911. Pettigrew's dream was too big. Despite the long line of wagons of wheat that had inspired Pettigrew's idea for the mill, the region was unable to provide sufficient wheat "at reasonable prices" to satisfy the mill's ravenous appetite. (R. F. Pettigrew Papers, Historical Writings; Bailey, 382)

In 1888 (November 5) the *Daily Argus Leader* reprinted an article on Sioux Falls from the *St. Paul Pioneer Press.* The Minnesota paper reported that "the growth of the city has come about largely because of the development of its stone interests, and because of the faith that the lines of small manufacturers already established and the infant jobbing interests would be greatly multiplied in consequence of her natural and acquired advantages." The writer had summed it up well. Certainly one of the major industries of the 1880s was its stone quarries. Blessed with an inexhaustible supply of extremely durable and attractive quartzite, it was rail transportation that made quarrying a major local industry. Col. J. H. Drake of St. Paul opened the first quarry in Sioux Falls in 1883 on the east side and soon after another was begun about two miles southeast of the city. By the end of the decade a number of stone quarries were operating in and around Sioux Falls, but the largest quarry development occurred in 1887 when the East Sioux Falls quarries were opened. Served by the Illinois Central Railroad, the quarry company constructed East Sioux Falls as a company town to house the rapidly growing army of stone-cutters and quarrymen it employed. By 1890 it employed nearly five hundred men and had a monthly payroll of twenty thousand dollars.

Sioux quartzite, as it was termed, became a favorite building material for the new business blocks, residences and public buildings erected in Sioux Falls in the 1880s and 1890s. It was also shipped to Chicago, St. Louis, Omaha, and other midwestern cities for building and for street paving. When Sioux Falls began paving its streets in 1888 it naturally used local quartzite paving stones.

Many other industries flourished in Sioux Falls during the 1880s. The Cascade Mill, built in 1878, operated as a flour mill and in 1887 added an electric generating plant to supply power to businesses, residences and public streets. In 1875 a brewery was begun on the North Main Avenue hill and it grew and prospered even through state prohibition in the early 1890s. A pork-packing plant began operations in 1883 just across the river from the downtown area. Its success made its presence intolerable; and so it moved, at the city council's insistence, to a site next to the river below the falls. Three yards were opened to manufacture pressed brick which was used to construct many local homes and businesses, and in 1883 the five Pankow brothers opened their iron foundry and machine shop. In 1884 Colonel Drake expanded his stone business by opening a polishing works at the second falls. There were also a host of smaller establishments including a wagon and plow works,

QUEEN BEE MILL.

OPERATING DEPARTMENT

FLOUR.

This Sioux Falls Weekly Press *advertisement in April 27, 1882 indicates the Queen Bee was struggling to stay in business.*

The worst flood in the history of Sioux Falls occurred in 1881 following the heaviest winter snowfall the region had experienced. When the ice finally broke in April, the Big Sioux River rose over fifteen feet above normal to flood most of the downtown area. With the raising of the grade on Phillips Avenue and the building of the diversion ditches and spillway in 1908, the threat of floods was reduced, but floods continued to cause major damage until the completion of levees and a new diversion system in 1960. Center for Western Studies photo

The Queen Bee Mill opened in 1881 only to close in 1883. Apparently there was not enough wheat available at reasonable prices in the area to keep it running profitably. Center for Western Studies photo

bottling works, marble works, vinegar factory, creameries and two cigar factories.

Schools and colleges are a type of industry, and Sioux Falls business leaders worked hard and contributed generously to get them located in the community. It was a good investment for the city, for colleges brought people to the community and gave it prestige. In 1881 when the Baptists of southern Dakota decided to open a college, Sioux Falls offered them six thousand dollars in cash and a free building site if they located the school here. The offer was accepted and in September, 1883, the Dakota Collegiate Institute, later to become Sioux Falls College, opened its doors. A year later, in 1884, the community agreed to provide ten thousand dollars in cash and land to Bishop William H. Hare of the Episcopal Diocese to induce him to construct All Saints School in the city. And in 1889, when the Norwegian Evangelical Lutheran Synod proposed to establish a Lutheran Normal Training School, local citizens raised fifty-six hundred dollars and Pettigrew and Tate donated four acres of land to make sure it was located in Sioux Falls.

By the end of the decade the pace of growth was matched only by the unbounded faith of local leaders in an even brighter future for their city. On July 12, 1889, the *Argus Leader* wrote, "There can now be little doubt but Sioux Falls' future as one of the greatest cities in the greater Northwest is not only within the range of possibility but of probability as well." The article went on to survey the building boom then in progress and to speculate about where the "business center" of the city would finally be fixed. It was currently where it had always been—at the corner of Ninth Street and Phillips Avenue. But the new County Court House being erected at Sixth and Main and the rash of new construction it was sparking on north Main Avenue and on Sixth Street seemed to indicate the city's center might be moving further north. Six large business blocks were planned for sites around the courthouse to "keep it from getting lonesome." These were to be office buildings for those wishing to be close to the traffic of county business and wholesale warehouses for businesses that needed to be close to the services of the Milwaukee Freight Yards.

Sioux Falls's rapid growth in the 1880s did not just happen. City leaders worked continuously and energetically to make it happen. On December 16, 1887, the *Argus Leader* announced a meeting that night at Pettigrew and Tate's office "to advertise Sioux Falls...." The purpose of the meeting was to take "steps towards advertising Sioux Falls abroad." Sioux Falls, the paper asserted was "just on a turning point between a town and a city and the action taken by her business men during the next year [would be] of vital importance. Now is the time, the *Argus* declared, "to boom the city." Many booming tactics were used. Ads were placed in eastern newspapers, brochures and pamphlets were printed and distributed, and personal contacts were used to their fullest.

Several promotional pamphlets were prepared in the 1880s and 1890s. On December 19, 1889, for instance, the *Argus Leader* announced the publication of a "handsome new book" entitled *Sioux Falls, the Queen City of South Dakota* written by Rev. J. H. Mooers. The article described the thirty-two page, ten-by-twelve-inch book as having "put in an exceedingly telling and attractive way a description of the natural advantages, the trade connections, and the rustling qualities which have built up Sioux Falls." The book was written, said the *Argus Leader* for "spreading the gospel of Sioux Falls through the East." It cost only two cents to send it through the mail, and the newspaper declared the book "should be scattered over the East by the thousands." Within a month the first printing was exhausted and a second ordered. On January 10, 1890, the *Argus Leader* reported that one real estate man had "sold eight thousand dollars worth of property through the books already." Orders for the book had been received "from many businessmen and speculators in the East and these orders," it said, "[would] be supplied first." The books cost twenty-five cents a copy and the *Argus* encouraged its readers to "place your order early."

Eastern investors, who came to see if the promotional hype was true, were generally impressed. On June 15, 1889, the *Argus Leader* quoted a visitor from Maine as saying, "I am more than ever pleased with Sioux Falls after seeing it. Hearing of it was convincing, but seeing it is always much more satisfactory. I confidently believe," declared the Maine investor, "from what experience teaches me that Sioux Falls is certainly destined to be the Minneapolis and St. Paul of this country, if not its Chicago."

Richard Pettigrew was doing his part to make that prophecy become a reality. As always his ideas were of grand proportions. In 1888 Pettigrew launched plans to create an industrial suburb to be called South

This early advertisement for the Heynsohn Brothers Minnehaha Spring shows the many uses found for the spring water. This was also a popular spa for eastern visitors waiting ninety days for their divorces. The Heynsohn's bottled water was a popular seller as the quality of the city's water, taken from the river, became poorer. Center for Western Studies photo

Sioux Falls. The *Argus Leader* reported on December 22, 1888, that the "prime object of this town is manufacture." Pettigrew raised the money to launch this ambitious enterprise from investors in Maine, and during the next three years he succeeded in stocking his industrial suburb with a woolen mill, an axle grease factory, a soap factory and a four-story cornstarch factory. The suburb was connected to Sioux Falls by Pettigrew, and Tate's trolley line, and their South Sioux Falls Railroad and Rapid Transit Company linked it to the railroad yards in Sioux Falls.

The crowning jewel of Pettigrew's manufacturing suburb was to be the South Sioux Falls Stockyards and Packing Plant. In the summer of 1889 Pettigrew hosted fourteen investors from Maine in Sioux Falls while he sold them his vision of the stockyard and packing plant. After two weeks the Sioux Falls Stockyards Company was chartered and by September one million dollars of stock had been sold. By March architectural plans were completed for a six-story main building 436 feet long and 160 feet wide and a second one three stories high and 50 by 80 feet. Construction began in May and by the time the construction season ended that winter a great deal of progress had occurred.

Unfortunately in 1891 the economy began its slide toward the Panic and Depression of 1893, and investment money dried up. Construction ceased until 1895 when another group bought out Pettigrew and his investors and completed the plant. The depression resumed in 1896, however, and the packing plant failed to begin operations. In 1899 the plant, under new ownership, operated for only a month before closing forever. A city-sponsored WPA project dismantled the plant buildings in 1939.

"West side rustlers," as the *Argus Leader* styled them, in 1890 formed the Sioux Falls Improvement Company to develop a second industrial suburb called West Sioux Falls. They hoped to attract industries by offering free building sites and good transportation facilities. They would make their money by selling residential lots to the one to two thousand factory workers they expected would be employed. They were in essence booming a new townsite. Before the onslaught of the depression in 1893 this group managed to establish three factories on their property: a mortising machine factory, an oatmeal mill and a wagon and carriage works. By 1894 all three factories were standing idle, victims of the hard times.

The bright optimism of the 1880s faded into dark

depression in the 1890s. Industrial suburbs and factories closed, businesses failed and speculators were unable to get money to keep their projects alive. Pettigrew and many other Sioux Falls boomers lost the fortunes they had amassed during the good times before 1893. Political fortune, too, failed to shine on Pettigrew in the 1890s. He threw his lot with the Populists, alienated the Republican party that had elected him to the United States Senate, and began his gradual transformation from a frontier Republican to a Socialist admirer of the Russian Revolution. Still, from his seat in the Senate, Pettigrew continued to help Sioux Falls. Through his efforts Congress appropriated funds to build the Federal Courthouse and post office building at Twelfth Street and Phillips Avenue in 1895. And it was he who insisted it be built of Sioux Falls quartzite.

In the 1890s, when most other local industries waned or failed, the divorce business continued to provide Sioux Falls a steady if inadequate income. Liberal grounds for divorce and a ninety-day residence requirement in the 1880s had made Dakota attractive to residents of eastern states where divorce was difficult if not impossible to obtain. As the largest and most comfortable city in Dakota, Sioux Falls had developed a sizeable trade in divorce during territorial days. In 1889, however, came statehood and with it a new six-month residency requirement for divorce. The business fell off sharply until 1893 when increased requirements in other states caused the divorce trade to return to South Dakota and to Sioux Falls. The divorce trade was a boon to the legal profession, of course, but it also benefitted the entire town. People spent six months in order to meet the residency requirement and obtain their divorce. That meant they rented hotel rooms, stayed in boarding houses or rented rooms in private homes. Some of the well-to-do bought houses and brought servants and other amenities of life to which they were accustomed back east. They demanded high fashion and quality goods in the local stores and supported theaters and other diversions. In short, they spent money in the town when money was not plentiful. City residents generally disapproved of "divorsays," as they were termed, but during the 1890s no effort was made to discourage the business.

In 1897 good times returned and with it a new optimism for the future began to emerge. Business leaders renewed the boosterism that had worked so well in the 1880s, and again it produced results.

Independence Day
At Sioux Falls, July 4, '82.

PROGRAMME:
SALUTE OF 13 GUNS AT SUNRISE

PROCESSION:

At 10 o'clock, formed at intersection of Main and Ninth Streets, thence, under direction of the Marshals to the Island. The procession will be arranged as follows:

President of the Day,
Orators,
Chaplain, and Reader of Declaration of Independence,
Flandrau Brass Band.
Members of Village Board of Trustees.
Sioux Falls Fire Co. No. 1,
Car, containing 40 Young Ladies. Representing the Goddess of Liberty, the States of the Union, and the Territory of Dakota.
Vocal Quartette,
Chorus of 100 Juveniles.
Citizens and Visitors on Foot,
Queen City Cornet Band.
Display of Business Houses and Manufactures.
Citizens and Visitors in Carriages,

AT THE ISLAND.

Called to order by President of the Day, M. Grigsby, Esq.
Music by the Queen City Cornet Band, on the Grand Stand.
Prayer by Rev. J. N. McLoney, Chaplain.
"AMERICA," by a Chorus of 100 Children, under the direction of R. J. Wells.
Reading Declaration of Independence, by Prof. S. E. Young.
"SOLDIER'S CHORUS," by R. J. Wells, E. M. Hills,
H. A. Fairbanks, and E. A. Sherman.
Oration, by C. H. Winsor, Esq.
"RED WHITE AND BLUE," by Juvenile Chorus,
Music by the Flandrau Band,
Oration, by Major T. S. Free,
Singing by the Quartette, audience joining in full Chorus,
DINNER.

Pigeon and Glass Ball Shooting, all day, (except during the procession, and formal exercises on the island), commencing at 8 o'clock, under the auspices of the Sioux Falls Gun Club, at the grounds on the plateau, Southwest of town.

PRIZES, - - $700.00.

TUB RACE on river, below pontoon bridge, at 2 o'clock, for a prize of TEN DOLLARS.
GREASED POLE on the island, at 2:30, for a prize of $5.

BASE BALL MATCH,

Between Flandrau and Sioux Falls Clubs, on plateau near Shooting Grounds at 4 o'clock, for prize of $25.
PONY RACE on plateau, near Shooting Grounds, at 5 o'clock, for TEN DOLLARS SWEEPSTAKES, free for all.

FIREWORKS.

The display of Fireworks will begin at 9 o'clock, on the hillside, west of the island, and will include the following exhibitions, among others: "Welcome," "Crystal Waterfall," Eruption of Mt. Vesurius," "Evening Star," "Revolving Sun," "Gypsy Dance," portraits of Washington and Garfield; immense meteoric balloons; a score of balloons of various designs, including figures of elephants, and other animals. The display will conclude with the exhibition piece, "Good Night."

BADGES.

The various Officers and Committees will be designated by appropriate badges, for the convenience of those who may desire to consult them.

NOTE.—The Queen Bee Mill will be open for visitors from 1 to 4 o'clock.

Independence Day was a big event in early Sioux Falls. The day of celebration began with a parade, but the main activities— speeches, picnics, band concerts, and fireworks—occurred at Seney Island. Center for Western Studies photo

The Cataract Hotel continued to be the best hotel in Sioux Falls. By 1878 the hotel had outgrown its first building, and a new brick structure was built north of it. Siouxland Heritage Museums photo

A volunteer Bucket Brigade was formed in 1877 as the first organized fire department in Sioux Falls. By the mid-1880s, when this picture was taken, the department had acquired the latest fire equipment, including a steam pumper and this hook and

ladder wagon. In the background is the Minnehaha Springs Bottling Works on the left and the original Hawthorne School, built in 1882, on the right. Center for Western Studies photo

The State Penitentiary, constructed in 1882, is shown here as it looked in the 1890s after prisoners had quarried stone to build the wall enclosing the prison yard. The entire structure was designed by Wallace A. Dow, with the first cell block being completed in 1882 and the warden's residence in 1884. R. F. Pettigrew, territorial delegate to Congress from 1881 to 1882, succeeded in getting a federal appropriation to construct the penitentiary at Sioux Falls. The story that Sioux Falls chose the penitentiary over the state university, because they knew the state would need a prison but might never have a university, is a myth. Center for Western Studies photo

Prisoners are shown marching back to the penitentiary after a day of work in the state quarry in the 1880s. Besides quarrying rock and building much of the prison facilities, early prisoners produced shirts and twine. Production of license plates began in 1926. Center for Western Studies photo

The Hattie Phillips House at present day Terrace Park was completed in 1885 at a cost of nearly $50,000. The house was badly burned in 1908, acquired by the city along with the land to create Covell Park in 1916, and was finally razed in 1966. Mrs. Phillips was the wife of Dr. J. L. Phillips, founder of downtown Sioux Falls, and came to town with her husband in 1870, taking up residence in the officers' quarters of abandoned Fort Dakota. The Phillips soon after bought a house at the northwest corner of Eleventh and Phillips where they lived until after Dr. Phillips died in 1882. Center for Western Studies photo

Looking north on Phillips Avenue from Tenth Street, between 1878-1881, this view shows C. K. Howard's new store, on the left, and far down the street is the brick Cataract Hotel erected in 1878. Center for Western Studies photo

This view of Phillips Avenue, looking north from between Ninth and Tenth in 1884, shows the new Cataract Hotel (in the center) that was built in 1882. With the increase in population brought by the railroad after 1878, Phillips Avenue changed rapidly with multi-story stone and brick buildings replacing the smaller, original frame buildings. Siouxland Heritage Museums photo

St. Michael's Catholic Church was built in 1883, one of many original churches built in Sioux Falls in the boom period of the 1880s. In 1915 this building was razed to make room for St. Joseph's Cathedral. Center for Western Studies photo

The fire tower built in 1884 at Ninth and Dakota Avenue (present day site of City Hall) housed the fire bell that called out the volunteer fire department. In 1899 the bell was mounted in the old City Auditorium and in 1912 it was moved to the new Central Fire Station at Ninth and Minnesota Avenue. This picture, taken in 1885, shows the tower after it was struck by lightning. Today the bell stands in front of Central Fire Station at Ninth and Minnesota. Siouxland Heritage Museums photo

The Cataract Hotel is shown here in 1885, looking north on Phillips Avenue. In 1881 the Corson Brothers (Henry joined Harry in 1878) moved the original Cataract Building out into Ninth Street and continued business while they erected this impressive W. L. Dow designed hotel. Center for Western Studies photo

In 1884 E. A. Sherman built the Sherman Block on the southwest corner of Ninth and Main. This building housed county offices until the new court house was erected in 1890 and the post office until the

Federal Building was built in 1895. In 1898 the Sherman Block was converted into the New Theatre which provided entertainment for Sioux Falls citizens until it was razed in 1916. Sherman began

the development of Main Avenue in the 1880s when he constructed this building. Until then the Sioux Falls business district was confined to Phillips Avenue. Siouxland Heritage Museums photo

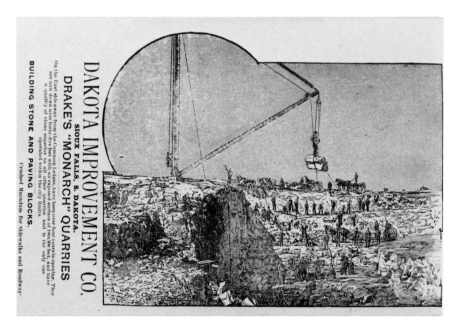

J. H. Drake of St. Paul opened the first quartzite quarry, the Monarch, in Sioux Falls in 1883. By 1890 there were five quarries in town quarrying stone for buildings and paving streets in Sioux Falls and many other cities throughout the Midwest. Center for Western Studies photo

The laying of the cornerstone of the first Masonic Temple took place at Tenth and Phillips in 1883. This view shows Tenth Street looking west. On the hill to the right is the Cameron residence that would later house the city's first hospital, and to the left is the house removed to erect the Carnegie Library Building in 1903. Photo from the History of Minnehaha Lodge, *volume 5*

The Masonic Temple, completed in 1884, contained retail shops on the ground floor, offices on the second, and lodge rooms on the third. In 1905 the building became known as the Peck Block when the masonic lodge moved to its new building on Tenth between Main and Dakota. The Minnehaha National Bank was in this building from 1898 until 1929 when it changed its name to the First National Bank and moved into its own building near Ninth and Phillips. First National Bank photo

Looking southwest from the Masonic Temple in 1883-84, this view shows the First Methodist Church on the left, built in 1881 at Eleventh and Main. At the upper center just to the right of Central School is St. Olaf Lutheran Church, forerunner to First Lutheran Church, and on the far right is the Congregational Church. Although many congregations were formed in the early 1870s, services were generally held in homes until they could afford to construct churches in the late 1870s and 1880s. Center for Western Studies photo

All Saints School, designed by local architect, W. L. Dow, was built in 1884. Located in Sioux Falls because of a gift of ten thousand dollars from its citizens, the school was originally a girl's school with programs through high school. Center for Western Studies photo

Bishop William Hobart Hare came to Dakota in 1873 as the Episcopal missionary bishop of Niobrara, the area of Dakota Territory. For ten years he spread the gospel and established schools among the Lakota Indians, but the Dakota boom of the late 1870s and early 1880s brought thousands of white settlers to Dakota. In 1884 the Episcopal church created the Diocese of Southern Dakota and elected Hare as bishop. At this time he chose Sioux Falls as his episcopal residence and built All Saints School as a boarding school for the daughters of his missionaries among the Indians. Bishop Hare was also instrumental in getting the divorce residency laws changed from six months to one year in 1908, effectively ending the divorce business in Sioux Falls. Center for Western Studies photo

39

This view looks south on Main Avenue from above the Sioux Falls Brewery and Malt Works in 1885. The brewery survived state prohibition in the early 1890s and from 1917 to 1918, but not National Prohibition after 1919. All Saints School can be seen in the distance. Center for Western Studies photo

The main building at the "South Dakota School for the Deaf and Mute" (its nineteenth-century name) is shown here in 1884. It was built that year to replace the original frame building that housed the school when it began in 1881 with five students. Siouxland Heritage Museums photo

The Drake Polishing Works was built by J. H. Drake in 1883-84 at the second falls just north of the Queen Bee Mill. Built to polish quartzite from Drake's Monarch Quarry and petrified wood from Arizona, the plant ceased operation early in this century. Center for Western studies photo

The "South Dakota School for the Deaf and Mute" barn and stable was built in 1886 when courses in farming and dairying were added to the original curriculum of printing, carpentry, and tinning. Center for Western Studies photo

41

The South Dakota School for the Deaf is shown here as it looked in the late 1890s. From left to right: boys dormitory, power plant, administration building, barn, and manual training building. All the school's buildings were designed by W. L. Dow and built on land given by E. A. Sherman. Siouxland Heritage Museum photo

This view looks south from the Cataract Hotel on Ninth and Phillips in about 1886. For some reason, possibly because of the flood danger, the east side of Phillips Avenue developed more slowly than the west side. The east side retained small wooden buildings long after they were virtually non-existent on the west side of the street. Siouxland Heritage Museums photo

This ad for the ancestor of the First National Bank appeared shortly after it first opened in 1885. Sioux Falls Daily Press, *January 6, 1886*

Meredith Hall, the original building of Sioux Falls College, was built in 1883. The Baptist school, known as "Sioux Falls University" until 1898, came to Sioux *Falls because of a six thousand dollar gift from the citizens of Sioux Falls. Named after the school's first president, Rev. E. B. Meredith, the building served the* *college until the mid-1960s. Center for Western Studies photo*

Wallace L. Dow, born in New Hampshire in 1844, was the foremost architect of Sioux Falls and the surrounding region for the last two decades of the nineteenth century. Territorial governor Nehemiah Ordway, also from New Hampshire, persuaded Dow to come to Dakota in 1880 to design the new public buildings being authorized by the legislature. Dow's design of the state penitentiary brought him to Sioux Falls in 1881 and, sensing the opportunities for him in the booming community, he decided to make it his *home. Dow was amazingly productive in the 1880s and early nineties as he designed dozens of the most prominent business, government and residential structures in Sioux Falls and eastern Dakota. Photo from Vol. 1, Issue 3 of* Prairie People

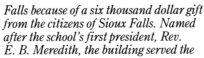

Dow's ad in the January 16, 1886 issue of the Sioux Falls Daily Press. *Dow came to South Dakota from New Hampshire in 1880*

The YMCA Block at Ninth and Main Avenue was the home of the Young Men's Christian Association from 1889 until 1893 when the organization disbanded, apparently a casualty of the financial panic and depression that struck that year. The YMCA did not revive until about twenty years later when efforts began to build the present building. The old YMCA Block was razed in 1938 to make room for the new Fantle's Store. Siouxland Heritage Museums photo

The Cascade Milling Company, on Eighth Street just east of the river, was a successful water-powered flour mill from 1877 until its demise in the early 1900s. In 1887, E. A. Sherman and others purchased the mill and proceeded to build the stone generating plant at the right. This steam powered plant produced the first alternating current electricity in Sioux Falls, allowing the use of Edison's recent invention—the incandescent light bulb. Center for Western Studies photo

The first explosion of the gas works occurred in October 1887. The Sioux Falls Gas Company had a total of three explosions before finally figuring out how to deal safely with this substance. The gas company, franchised by the city in 1886, furnished gas for street lighting until 1905 and for residential lighting for several years more. Siouxland Heritage Museums photo

This view of Minnesota Avenue looks south from Third Street in about 1892. Twenty years before, when Sioux Falls was a new settlement, there had been no trees anywhere but along the river. St. Michael's Catholic Church is at the far right with lumberman John Tuthill's residence just to the left of the church. Munce Brothers photo

In 1889 Ninth Street looked like this from Dakota Avenue. Germania Hall, built in 1880 and the site of the state constitutional conventions of 1883, 1885, and 1889, is at left, while next to it is the Metropolitan Block built in 1886. At the end of the block, the Cataract's tower can be seen. The only paved street at this point was Phillips from Fifth to Twelfth. Siouxland Heritage Museums photo

Looking southwest from the Phillips House Hotel on the east side at Eighth and Reid Avenue in 1890, the Rock Island Depot, Masonic Temple, and Central School are all visible. Siouxland Heritage Museums photo

The Burlington, Cedar Rapids and Northern Railroad Depot, later the Rock Island, as it appeared at Tenth and First Avenue in 1886. Made of quartzite and one of the nicest depots in Sioux Falls, it was remodeled into a restaurant after being abandoned in 1970. Center for Western Studies photo

The Merchants Hotel, at Sixth and Phillips, a popular hotel in Sioux Falls, was built in 1878. It was almost destroyed by the flood of 1881, when they had to chop a hole in the wall to let the current run through. Destroyed by fire in 1912, the Merchants was replaced by the Albert House. Center for Western Studies photo

George Burnside was one of the better
known undertakers in Sioux Falls, as well
as the owner of a first class hack service.
But he was probably best known for being
mayor of Sioux Falls for twenty-six years
starting in 1900. His administration
decided many issues that affect the city
to this day, including the municipal or
private ownership of utilities and the
development of the city parks. Center for
Western Studies photo

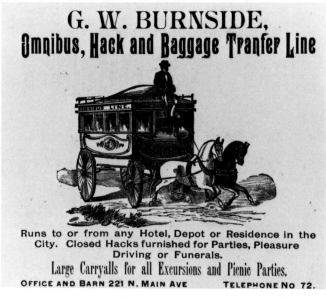

The L. T. Dunning residence at Eighth
and Duluth is shown here about 1890.
Lyman Dunning owned the drug store at
Eighth and Phillips from 1873 until his
death in 1920. His brother-in-law,
R. F. Pettigrew, built the house next door
after he got married in 1878 and lived
there until he moved to New York City in
1901. Center for Western Studies photo

Looking north from the Masonic Temple
in 1887, this photo shows R. F. Pettigrew's
street car line being built down Phillips
Avenue. This line, ultimately extending
for eight miles all the way to present day
Western Avenue and I-229, helped Pettigrew sell many residential lots he owned
along its route. The three story Norton-
Murray Building on the right was constructed during the previous year. Center
for Western Studies photo

This 1887 view of the city looks east from the roof of the A. C. Phillips house at Eighth Street and Duluth. The L. T. Dunning home is at the left, and Seney Island is clearly visible as the only area with a heavy growth of trees. Center for Western Studies photo

This view shows Seventh and Phillips looking south in 1887 as trolley tracks were being laid in front of the Van Brunt Building and the Commercial House (built in 1884), which operated under several names including the Teton until being razed in 1939 to make way for the Hollywood Theatre. At the upper left is the Cascade Mill. Siouxland Heritage Museums photo

The Sioux Falls Street Railroad operated from 1887 until 1896 but was never profitable. R. F. Pettigrew and his business partner, S. L. Tate, built the trolley line to boost the town and to sell real estate along its routes. At its high point the trolley line had eight miles of track, forty horses, six cars, and employed fourteen men. This particular car went from downtown railroad depots down Summit Avenue to Sioux Falls University, the Lutheran Normal School, and South Sioux Falls. The depression of 1893 caused the trolley to fail along with Pettigrew's other business ventures. Center for Western Studies photo

East Sioux Falls is shown here in the 1890s. Started in 1888 as a thriving company-owned quarrying town, East Sioux Falls was located along present-day Highway 38 near the Big Sioux River. At its peak in 1891 East Sioux Falls had slightly more than six hundred residents. The Illinois Central Railroad, the transporter of its product, was key to the quarry town's existence. In 1890 a trolley line was constructed to East Sioux Falls from downtown Sioux Falls. The community started to die during the Depression of 1893 to 1897 and was finally ended by the shortage of railroad cars during World War I. Some buildings and the huge quarry pits still remain today. Siouxland Heritage Museums photo

Many stone cutters from Scotland, Wales and Scandinavia were attracted to Sioux Falls in the 1880s and 1890s to work as stonecutters in the city's many quarries. This highly skilled work on nature's second hardest substance employed hundreds at its peak in the early 1890s. Later the industry declined when quartzite was replaced by other materials for building and paving. These men are paving-block cutters at the East Sioux Falls quarry about 1890. Center for Western Studies photo

This 1889 view of the Fourth of July in Sioux Falls looks north on Phillips from Eleventh Street, the southern end of the business district. The Cataract Hotel had just expanded again with the addition of a fourth floor, and Pettigrew's trolley is at the bottom left. Siouxland Heritage Museums photo

The new Hollister-Beveridge Block and the Cataract Hotel were located on Ninth Street in 1890. This office building was a Sioux Falls landmark until being razed in 1973. Pettigrew had his office here in the 1890s. Center for Western Studies photo

The original Lincoln School is shown here as it looked in about 1890. This quartzite structure, designed by W. L. Dow in 1888 with only six rooms, was soon outgrown. It was razed in 1915 and replaced by a one story building of the same name. Center for Western Studies photo

The William A. Dow residence, was located at 421 South Duluth in this 1890 photo. The house was undoubtedly designed by his brother, Wallace L. Dow, the architect. William Dow was a heating contractor. Siouxland Heritage Museums photo

The original Lutheran Normal School building was built in 1889. R. F. Pettigrew gave four acres of land and Sioux Falls donated five thousand dollars to establish the Normal School in Sioux Falls. In 1918, following a Lutheran Church merger, Augustana College was moved to Sioux Falls from Canton and the united schools became Augustana College. Center for Western Studies photo

Looking south on Phillips Avenue from Eighth in 1889, this photo shows an addition being built to the William Van Eps Block at the corner of Eighth and Phillips. The corner building, built in 1886 to replace Van Eps's original store, was a general merchandise store and office building until it was razed in 1969. Siouxland Heritage Museums photo

Amund Mikkelsen, born in Norway, was called by the Lutheran church in 1889 to run the new Lutheran Normal School in Sioux Falls. He served as principal, chaplain, and instructor at the school for many years and led in establishing the first hospital in Sioux Falls in 1894. Center for Western Studies photo

Bishop Martin Marty, born in Switzerland in 1834, came to Dakota Territory in 1876 as a missionary to the Indians of the Standing Rock Agency. He was named bishop of all of Dakota Territory in 1879, and in 1889, when the Catholic Church created the Diocese of South Dakota, Marty became its first bishop. Photo from Dana Bailey's History of Minnehaha County

The Bishop Martin Marty residence was built at the east end of the Twenty-first Street Boulevard in 1890 when the bishop chose Sioux Falls as the headquarters for the Catholic Diocese of South Dakota. Bishop O'Gorman replaced Marty in 1895 and lived there until his death in 1921. Bishop O'Gorman is perhaps best known for his leadership in building McKennan Hospital in 1911. The house was given to the hospital in 1944 and razed for expansion in 1973. Center for Western Studies photo

This view looks northwest from the Phillips House Hotel in 1890-91. Directly in front is the Illinois Central Depot built in 1887 at a cost of forty-eight thousand dollars. The court house tower can be seen, partially completed, in the background. By this time there were five railroad lines into Sioux Falls and over ten thousand people. Center for Western Studies photo

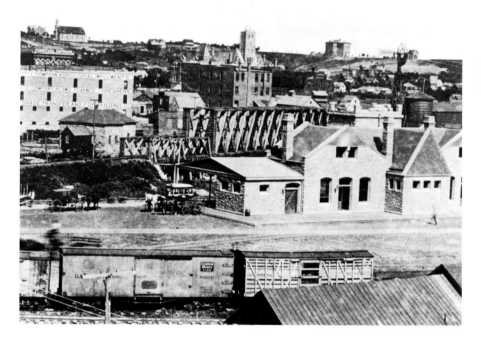

First Baptist Church on Eighth and Dakota was built in 1882. In the background is the new Minnehaha County Court House, before the clock was installed, which would indicate this picture was taken about 1891-92. Center for Western Studies photo

The Minnehaha County Court House is shown as it appeared in the 1890s. The old county jail, constructed in 1881-82, is just to its right. The court house, designed by W. L. Dow, was used for county offices and court rooms until the completion of the new court house in 1962. On September, 11, 1965 the Argus Leader ran an editorial which said in part: "The public would be better served by razing the court house and converting the space to public parking."

"The new court house is a beautiful structure but it needs some breathing space on both the east and west sides." Fortunately, the editor's advice was not taken, and today this beautiful building is the Old Court House Museum. Siouxland Heritage Museums photo

Looking north on Main Avenue from Tenth in 1889, this photo shows the Union Trust Bank Building on the left, which was built in 1888 and razed in 1965 to make way for a new bank building. The building next to it, the Odd Fellows Hall built in 1889 by R. F. Pettigrew, still stands. Center for Western Studies photo

Looking north from the new post office at Twelfth and Phillips in about 1895 shows there was little development south of Tenth. One of Pettigrew's horse drawn trolleys is heading north on Phillips Avenue. Center for Western Studies photo

The Scott and Thompson Machinery Company was located on east Seventh Street in the early nineties. The wagons in the foreground are loaded with McCormick reapers on their way to local farms. The firm did not survive the depression of 1893. Siouxland Heritage Museums photo

This view looks south on Main from Eighth in about 1898. The one story building on the right is the Argus Leader Building. The Argus Leader, one of several papers in Sioux Falls at the time, was originally a weekly Democratic newspaper that resulted from a merger of the Leader from 1883 and the Argus from 1881. It switched to the Republican party during the 1896 McKinley election. Up the street is the Sherman Block that had been remodeled and enlarged to create the New Theatre. Center for Western Studies photo

56

On the right, in this 1895 view toward the south from Eighth and Main, is the Syndicate Block. This W. L. Dow structure was built with the efforts of many of the city's leading citizens in 1890 in an effort to promote Main Avenue as an important business street. In 1909 Joe Kirby purchased the building, and it became known as the Western Surety Building until it was razed in 1962 to make room for the First Bank of South Dakota. Siouxland Heritage Museums photo

This Lad the Tailor advertisement, from about 1900, attempts to appeal to the fashion consciousness of the Sioux Falls theatre-going crowd. Sioux Falls had several theatres in the nineteenth and early twentieth centuries. At this time the New Theatre, the Booth Theatre on Eighth, and Germania Hall all booked the many traveling acts that regularly stopped in Sioux Falls. The coming of motion pictures in the late teens gradually ended the popularity of live theater in the city. Center for Western Studies photo

Calvary Episcopal Cathedral was located at Thirteenth and Main in the early nineties. The first church structure in Sioux Falls, built in 1872, was an Episcopal Church at Ninth and Main. In 1888 Bishop Hare persuaded the eastern millionaire John Jacob Astor to finance the construction of this new cathedral church in memory of Astor's late wife Augusta. It was named the Church of Saint Augusta when constructed in 1889, but it had no congregation until Hare invited the Calvary congregation to leave its old building for this new one. Hence it became Calvary Cathedral. Center for Western Studies photo

All Souls Unitarian Church was built in 1888-89 at Twelfth and Dakota through the leadership of Pastor Caroline Bartlett and member Mrs. Eliza Wilkes. The congregation, unable to support a pastor in the depression of the 1890s, disbanded. In 1899, W. H. Lyon, who then owned the building, donated it to the city for a public library until the completion of the Carnegie Library in 1903. The building was then used as a church until being razed in 1971. Center for Western Studies photo

58

The Cataract Hotel dining room is shown here shortly before the turn of the century. The Cataract maintained its early reputation as the finest place to stay and dine in Sioux Falls. It catered to well-to-do travelers and especially to those who came to Sioux Falls to obtain a divorce. A story is told about the apparently wealthy woman who checked into the Cataract in the late 1890s and passed the word that she would interview lawyers that evening at seven o'clock to select one to handle her divorce proceedings. The lawyers began to assemble in the lobby and were told there would be a slight delay. They drifted into the bar and the evening passed until someone decided to go upstairs to find out when the interviews would begin. It was discovered that the "lady" had left by the back stairs, and it was obvious there would be no interviews. Later that night as the Cataract bar was closing, one of the loitering attorneys overheard one bartender say to the other, "That interview story of yours was the best idea for business we've had in a long time." Center for Western Studies photo

The Sioux Falls Linen Mill, just south of the present day John Morrell Packing Plant, was built in 1890-91. It ran for only a few years, another victim of the 1893 depression. The building served briefly as a pickling works, but in 1905 it became part of the Dakota or Green Meat Packing Plant. In 1909 the John Morrell Company purchased the building when it began operations in Sioux Falls. The building was razed in 1949. Center for Western Studies photo

The South Dakota Rapid Transit and Rail-road Company, built in 1890, was the first electric trolley in South Dakota. The line ran for six miles from the west side of Tenth Street Viaduct to East Sioux Falls for three years, but the decline of East Sioux Falls after 1893 caused it to cease operations. *Siouxland Heritage Museums photo*

A circus parade took place in Sioux Falls on Eighth and Phillips in the late 1890s. The circus, after unloading from the train, always paraded down Phillips Avenue as it headed toward the circus grounds between Eighth and Tenth streets on the east side of the river. Center for Western Studies photo Studies photo

A circus performance in progress at the East Side circus grounds in the 1890s. Note the midway tents off on the right and the Tenth Street Viaduct on the left. Photo from Vol. 4, Issue 4 of Prairie People

In 1888 R. F. Pettigrew and his partner S. L. Tate launched the industrial suburb of South Sioux Falls. They succeeded in attracting several industries including a woolen mill (background on the right), a soap factory, an axle grease factory, and a cornstarch factory. None of these industries survived more than a few years before closing. South Sioux Falls also boasted a hotel called the Buffalo Park Hotel seen on the left and named after the nearby Buffalo Park that contained a herd of seventeen buffalo. In the foreground is the foundation for a Presbyterian Church that was never built. Located near the present day Western Avenue and I-229, the town was linked to downtown Sioux Falls by Pettigrew's horse drawn trolley line. Center for Western Studies photo

The cornstarch factory in South Sioux Falls, which opened in 1892, produced six varieties of cornstarch, but operated for only a few months. This factory, like the others in South Sioux Falls, never reopened after the 1893 depression. Center for Western Studies photo

R. F. PETTIGREW, *President.*   S. L. TATE *Vice Pres. and Treas.*

Pioneer Soap Company of Dakota

SIOUX FALLS, SOUTH DAKOTA.

MANUFACTURE FULL LINES IN

LAUNDRY AND TOILET SOAPS

E. McBRIDE, Secretary and General Manager.

J. G. STRAHON,

This advertisement for the South Sioux Falls soap factory, appeared in the three page South Sioux Falls section of the 1890-91 Sioux Falls City Directory. The factory burned to the ground in March 1892 before the depression could close it like its neighboring factories. There was no South Sioux Falls section in the 1893-94 city directory. Center for Western Studies photo

R. F. Pettigrew's office was located in the Hollister Building next door to the Cataract Hotel on Ninth Street during the early 1890s. The room is filled with local produce that might convince clients to buy land or invest money in the area. There are bolts of cloth from the South Sioux Falls Woolen Mill, flour from the Pettigrew-owned St. Olaf Mill at Baltic, and lots of corn and other produce. Note Pettigrew's travelling desk in the corner. This desk is now on display in the Pettigrew museum. Siouxland Heritage Museums photo

This giant meatpacking plant in South Sioux Falls was begun by R. F. Pettigrew and investors from Maine in 1889. It was located just west of the river and north of Forty-first Street. The plant was actually not finished by the end of 1890 and Pettigrew was forced to sell the unfinished plant to a new group of owners who completed it in 1895. This group could go no further, and the plant stood idle until 1899 when a third group of investors bought it and began meat processing. After operating one month, legal action from previous investors closed the plant forever. The building was dismantled in 1939 as a city sponsored WPA project, and the stone was used in numerous city parks, notably along the road in Falls Park. Center for Western Studies photo

The Chicago Machine Works was built in 1890 as part of the projected industrial suburb of West Sioux Falls near the present W. H. Lyons Fairgrounds. West Sioux Falls also included an oatmeal mill and a wagon factory before the 1893 depression closed them down. In 1895 a tornado destroyed all the buildings except the oatmeal mill. Center for Western Studies photo

The West Sioux Falls Oatmeal Mill, erected in 1891, was built in response to the national oatmeal health-food craze of the time. But like the rest of West Sioux Falls it closed during the financial panic of 1893. Center for Western Studies photo

Irving High School at the corner of Eleventh and Spring, seen here in the late 1890s, was the predecessor to Washington High School, built in 1907. The building was originally erected in 1890 as St. Rose Academy, a Catholic school for grades one through twelve. The school closed in 1895, apparently because of a dispute between the priest of St. Michael's Church and the Ursuline Sisters who ran the school. That summer the Sioux Falls Public School District bought the building for a high school and added stone veneer to the frame structure. In 1901 the school was renamed McKinley High School as a memorial to the slain president. When the north wing of Washington High was completed in 1907, the building was converted to Irving Elementary School. It was razed in 1935-36 when a WPA project erected the present Irving School. Center for Western Studies photo

A Lincoln Elementary School classroom is shown here in 1891. Sioux Falls grew so rapidly in the 1880s that it was a real struggle for the public school system to erect schools fast enough to keep up. Free textbooks were not provided to Sioux Falls students until 1913. W. Don Erickson photo

The interior of the Williams Cigar Store is shown here in the 1890s. The store, located on Phillips Avenue, sold mainly cigars, chewing tobacco, and snuff. Cigars were far more popular than cigarettes at the time. Even as late as the 1920s the average man in Sioux Falls smoked three cigars a day. At the time this picture was taken there were three cigar factories in Sioux Falls. Center for Western Studies photo

This picture of the Keeley Institute was taken shortly after its completion in 1891. Built by the Heynsohn Brothers, the Institute used the Keeley Method to cure alcoholism and drug addiction. Heynsohn Spring Water was piped into the building from the hillside behind it. At the time, alcohol abuse was even more severe than it is today, and morphine addiction was quite common as it was legally available. The Institute closed in 1919 following the enactment by Congress of national prohibition. Center for Western Studies photo

This is the interior of the Fantle Brothers Department Store about 1900. Most clothing was still sewn at home at this time. Customers sat on stools while clerks waited on them. Self-service was unknown. Fantle Brothers started in 1896 with a stock of three thousand dollars. Center for Western Studies photo

The Granite Cutters' National Union, Sioux Falls branch, was formed in 1889. This union reached a peak membership of about one hundred in 1892 but was disbanded in 1895 because of the economic downturn. These members are standing in front of the new post office while it was under construction in 1895. Besides the Granite Cutters, other early unions included the Typographical Union, the Cigar-Makers Union, the Retail Clerks Union, and the Barbers Union. Center for Western Studies photo

Willow Dale Mansion, a brothel, stood south of present day Twelfth Street and west of the river. Seen here during the flood of 1892, it was one of several apparently well-patronized brothels that operated openly just outside the city limits throughout the 1880s and 1890s. The Argus Leader on August 29, 1889 reported, "there is one thriving business in Sioux Falls, at least, and that is what is called 'Willow Dale Mansion' or in other words Madame Doyle's bagnio west of town.
Hacks go through the western part of the city at all times of the day and night filled with drunken men and boys. It is becoming such a nuisance that property owners are beginning to get desperate." Center for Western Studies photo

The new Federal Building and Post Office at Twelfth and Phillips shortly after it was completed in 1895. Sen. R. F. Pettigrew introduced the bill in Congress that provided the funds. In 1913 a third floor was added, and in 1933 the eastern annex was built to cope with the increased postal and court needs. Center for Western Studies photo

The interior of the new Post Office is shown here in 1895. Note the spittoons on the floor. In 1966 postal operations were moved to the present building on Second Avenue. Center for Western Studies photo

The Chicago, Milwaukee and St. Paul Railroad Depot at Fifth and Phillips as it looked in about 1907. The Milwaukee Road absorbed the second and third rail companies to reach Sioux Falls, and it built this passenger and the nearby freight depots in 1894. This depot was replaced in 1946. Center for Western Studies photo

Mayor G. W. Burnside is sitting in the center of the front row of this meeting in the City Auditorium. The auditorium was used for basketball games, conventions, dances, and other meetings until the completion of the Coliseum in 1917. Center for Western Studies photo

The City Auditorium at Ninth and Dakota was built in 1898-99. In 1898 the Sioux Falls Business Men's League convinced the National Buttermaker's Association to hold its 1899 convention in the city. In the summer of 1898 the city realized it had no facility large enough to hold the convention. Moving quickly, the city commissioned W. L. Dow to design a combination auditorium and city hall, and it was erected in less than six months. Although the exterior was not stuccoed and city offices were not complete, the auditorium was ready for the buttermakers at the end of January 1899. This building and nearby Germania Hall (called Columbia Hall after World War I) were razed in 1934-35 to make room for the current city hall. Center for Western Studies photo

This view of Minnesota Avenue south from Eleventh Street in the late 1890s shows that it was still a quiet residential street. Commercial development on Minnesota Avenue near downtown began after 1914 but it did not bear heavy traffic until Highway 77 was graded and graveled in the 1920s. South Minnesota Avenue remained residential until it gradually became commercialized beginning in the 1950s. Center for Western Studies photo

Col. Melvin Grigsby, born in Wisconsin in 1845, came to Sioux Falls fresh out of law school in 1872. During the Civil War he had been captured by the Confederate Army and imprisoned in the infamous Andersonville Prison for six months. He later wrote of his wartime experiences in the book Smoked Yank. *At the outset of the Spanish-American War in 1898 Grigsby was given command of one of three special volunteer cowboy cavalry regiments authorized by Congress. Teddy Roosevelt's regiment made it to Cuba and glory, but Grigsby's Cowboys only got as far as Camp Thomas, Georgia, where several died from the unhealthy camp conditions. Although initially law partners, Grigsby and R. F. Pettigrew were bitter political and business rivals in the 1880s. Photo from George Kingsbury's* History of Dakota Territory, *vol. V*

This photo of Phillips Avenue looks north from Tenth Street in 1898. On the corner of Ninth and Phillips is the Edmison-Jamison Building. Designed by W. L. Dow and built in 1890, this six-story building had many lawyer tenants who wanted their office near the numerous divorce clients who stayed at the Cataract Hotel across the street. The parade is the First South Dakota Infantry Regiment that was mustered into federal service at Sioux Falls before departing for the Philippine Islands during the Spanish-American War. Center for Western Studies photo

On May 19, 1898, the First South Dakota
Infantry, United States Volunteers, was
mustered into federal service at the circus
grounds on the east side near present-day
Nelson Field. The regiment drilled until
May 29 when they left by train for the
West Coast, and more training before
embarking for the Philippine Islands.
Center for Western Studies photo

Railroads Build a City
1898 to 1918

Between 1878 and 1893 Sioux Falls business leaders had worked hard to build railroads that would make their city an important regional distribution and market center. They saw this as crucial to the future growth and prosperity of the city. In the post-depression period of 1898 to 1918 the strategy yielded its expected results, for the railroads did build the city. The railroads were the key to the city's success in the new century, for they made possible the rapid development of a large wholesale business in the city. In turn the wholesale distribution network in the surrounding region gave rise to regional manufacturing establishments in the city. And, of course, the railroads ran both ways. They not only distributed goods to the smaller cities and towns of the region, they brought agricultural produce and people to Sioux Falls. As a result Sioux Falls increasingly became what geographers term "a central place."

The wholesale and manufacturing business had begun in the 1880s and early 1890s, but the depression that began in 1893 not only stopped its growth but caused the failure of many promising business operations. In 1898 good times returned, and Sioux Falls was quick to make the most of it. A flurry of new wholesale houses and manufacturing establishments appeared which drew workers to the city. They in turn supported a revival of the city's retail trade. On January 3, 1900, the *Argus Leader* described the rebirth of business prosperity in the following words: "The year 1899 was a great year for Sioux Falls. Substantial growth was made along all lines. The wholesale and retail trade expanded to a point which made the bank clearings double those of 1898. The present houses filled up until it is estimated that fully one hundred

*Looking at this map from an 1898 Sioux
Falls promotional booklet, one could easily
believe that all railroads led to Sioux Falls.
This was not quite the case even though the
city did boast six railroad lines. Brookings,
Aberdeen and Watertown also had direct
lines that did not first stop in Sioux Falls
as the map suggests. It was true, however,
that Sioux Falls, because of these six lines,
was becoming a regional distributing
center. Center for Western Studies photo*

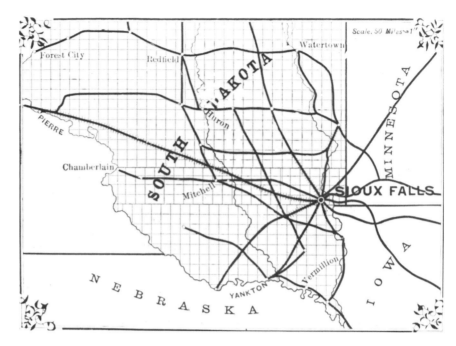

*In 1900, thanks to the influence of
R. F. Pettigrew, the Populist party held its
national convention in Sioux Falls to
nominate William Jennings Bryan as its
presidential candidate. This march was
written for this big event. Center for
Western Studies photo*

families are compelled to board or room in downtown blocks because residences cannot be secured though fifty new ones have been built. The vacant store rooms have likewise filled and streets which two or three years ago were almost deserted are now busy with trade."

The *Argus* writer asked rhetorically what had caused this "rush of new residents?" and then proceeded to explain it. First, he wrote, every existing business had expanded and hired employees to handle the increased trade. But even more important was the fact that "seventy new firms of various kinds and sizes have come in, occupying additional store and office room, employing more people and swelling the general tide of business." This included five wholesale houses and five manufacturers.

Two years later on January 21, 1902, the *Argus Leader* ran another report on the growth of business in the city. "Fifteen years ago," the article declared, "the wholesale interests of Sioux Falls amounted to but little...." But things had changed. There were now "twenty-three jobbing houses in Sioux Falls, which... employed 269 people in the house and 78 on the road. These houses aggregated a business of over four millions of dollars during the year 1901." The writer, however, felt the wholesale business of the city "has but just begun." And he was right. In the next two decades the wholesale business of the city did flourish as did manufacturing. Sioux Falls, as a result, experienced a greater population growth than ever before. By 1920 its population was two and one-half times larger than in 1900.

More than doubling in size in twenty years meant that Sioux Falls changed in many ways. New neighborhoods sprang up, people moved away from the center of the city as the business section expanded, congregations outgrew their churches and built new, larger ones, new schools were built to keep pace with the growing school population, the manufacturing and wholesale district north of the downtown area blossomed, and railroad freight yards expanded with sidings serving every warehouse and factory.

Downtown Sioux Falls changed noticeably as it increasingly served a larger resident population and became a regional shopping center as well. Old frame structures were replaced, new multi-story business and office structures were built, hotels and store buildings destroyed by fire were promptly replaced by larger modern structures, and outgrown and abandoned churches in the downtown area were converted to commercial use and eventually removed. In 1915, forty blocks of the business district became the "White Way" as a new system of illuminous arc street lights were installed.

The rapid growth of the city after 1900 soon made the need for public transportation evident, and in 1907 that need was met when street cars again began to operate on the city's streets. In that year Frank Moody Mills, seventy-six years old and having just sold the *Des Moines Register*, moved to Sioux Falls to found and operate the Sioux Falls Traction Company. Modern electric trolleys, not the horse drawn cars of Pettigrew's earlier venture, now connected the ever moving frontier of new residential construction to the downtown. By 1916 the company had installed sixteen miles of tracks serving most areas of the city, and one could ride the entire line for only five cents.

Even before the new trolley company began its operations in 1907, the rival means of transportation that would eventually put it out of business had appeared on city streets. In 1899 Harry C. Fenn brought the first automobile to Sioux Falls, and although leading citizens, including E. A. Sherman, spoke out against them because they endangered lives and property and would hurt the retail trade by scaring people away, the number of automobiles in Sioux Falls grew quickly. In 1903 the city already felt it was necessary to pass an ordinance to regulate the speed of these noisy and dangerous vehicles to seven miles per hour and four miles per hour when making corners. Two years later, when the state began requiring auto registration, there were already 480 in South Dakota. By 1920 this number had grown to over 112,000.

The automobile made an impact upon the city and its residents in several ways. Traffic laws and driving rules had to be established and enforced. Sioux Falls adopted an expanded automobile ordinance in 1909 that raised speed limits to ten miles per hour (eight around corners), set a minimum age for drivers, required mufflers and specifically proscribed "careless driving." In 1916 the city boasted of having "six semaphore, manufactured in Minneapolis, and of the same type as those used for traffic regulation in the Minnesota metropolis" as well as forty-five parking signs and two traffic officers. A photo of the police force in that year also reveals the city had a motorcycle patrolman. (*Illustrated Statistical and Descriptive*

The Spanish American War troop encampment near Nelson Field was named Camp Dewey after Adm. George Dewey's victory at Manila Bay on May 1, 1898. Center for Western Studies photo

Jonas H. Lien (1874-1899), brother of Sioux Falls mayor B. H. Lien, was the first Sioux Falls man killed in war. Lien Park is named in his honor and the black stone trim on the north side of Washington High, quarried in Lien Park, is a memorial to him. Photo from Charles A. Smith's Minnehaha County History

Report of the Government of Sioux Falls, South Dakota, 1916)

Automobile owners soon became a pressure group that lobbied for the improvement of streets and roads. The quartzite paving stones that surfaced business district streets were too rough for the faster moving automobiles, and beginning in 1914 they were replaced with smoother materials. Creosoted wood blocks were tried on Phillips Avenue, but concrete replaced paving stones on some streets while on others they were covered with asphalt.

The automobile also gave rise to a new segment of the city's business community. The first auto dealership appears in the 1903 city directory. By 1913 the number had risen to nine, and three years later it had more than doubled. There were twenty-nine dealers listed in the 1918 directory along with seventy-seven auto-related businesses ranging from tires to "auto repairers." The gas station also made its first appearance during this period.

Local dealerships appeared, merged and disappeared from year to year as the national auto industry matured and consolidated. But by 1917 the real take-off period began in Sioux Falls. In that year a quarter of a million dollars was spent in constructing dealership buildings, and this auto construction phase continued into 1919 when the Watkin and Leavitt Building, described by the *Argus Leader* as the "largest garage in the Northwest" opened at Ninth and Minnesota. Nearly a dozen of the new dealership garages were located within a block of the intersection of Ninth and Dakota. In its October 7, 1919, issue the *Argus Leader* summed up local developments well when it observed that "garages in an American city are about the most common building one can find."

76

Trolleys and autos made Sioux Falls citizens increasingly mobile and allowed the city to grow without residents losing ready access to the downtown for shopping and employment. Still, as the city grew the neighborhood corner store sprang up in residential areas to serve residents for whom it was inconvenient to travel downtown for groceries. The corner grocery would in time become the suburban shopping mall.

In the new century, city government wrestled with important issues relating to the needs of the rapidly growing community. Some issues were settled quickly. In August 1900, less than two months after the Cataract Hotel burned to the ground despite the efforts of the volunteer fire fighters, the city created its first paid, full-time fire department. Other issues, however, went unresolved for years as the city council argued, procrastinated or reversed itself. Issues of water, electricity, and sewer service are prime examples. Complaints about the quality of water furnished the community by the South Dakota Water Company, a private corporation using the river as its water source, led the city council to issue bonds in 1901 to create a municipal water system. Not until six years later, however, did the new water system begin operation from a well field north of town. The city council also decided to build its own municipal electric plant when its contract for street lighting with the Cascade Milling Company expired in 1901. Two steam driven generators were installed in an old canning factory north of the city to supply electricity for street lighting. This began a long controversy over whether the entire city should be supplied by private or public electric power. Neither side was able to win a clear victory, but in 1907 the Sioux Falls Light and Power Company began generating electricity from its new hydro plant north of the Queen Bee Mill and became the city's main source of electrical power. The City Light Plant, however, was maintained and expanded to light city streets and to maintain competition for the private company in the absence of public regulation of electric rates.

Sioux Falls city government, based on its charter of 1883, consisted of a mayor and council, with two aldermen elected from each ward. The inability of the city government to act decisively on important issues led several leading businessmen to begin a campaign to reform city government. Their model was the commission form of government created in Galveston, Texas, after a hurricane destroyed much of that city in 1900. The five-member full-time commission had promptly rebuilt Galveston without the customary squabblings and political maneuverings of the aldermanic form of city government. After narrowly losing in 1907, the reform forces succeeded in 1908 and Sioux Falls adopted the commission form of government. Five commissioners, elected at large as salaried, full-time officials, administered city government. Turbulence continued at city hall, however, and in 1913 Sioux Falls voted by a narrow margin to reduce the number of commissioners to three. This form of government continued until 1986 when the city again returned to a five person commission.

One of the most difficult issues for city government to resolve in this period was the construction of a public sewer system. An outside consultant in 1892 had drawn up a plan for a sewer system to handle street run-off in the business district, but by 1911 it was outdated and still not completed. In the meantime residential neighborhoods had been compelled to organize private sewer companies to build sewer lines.

Fireworks ignited in a store window of the Cataract Hotel Building in June 1900, and destroyed the structure completely. Although no one was killed in the fire, the ineffectiveness of the volunteer fire department in fighting the blaze caused the city to establish a full-time department by August of that year. Center for Western Studies photo

The new Cataract Hotel is shown here as it looked when completed in 1901. The Corson brothers started to rebuild immediately after the fire, and the new building was in keeping with the Cataract's long reputation as the finest hotel in the Dakota's. Center for Western Studies photo

The Children's Home at Tenth and Cliff Avenue, completed in 1903, was a refuge for homeless children until 1969. In 1973 the building was razed to make way for the Lewis Eastgate Store. Center for Western Studies photo

In 1912 the city commission finally adopted a new sewer construction plan that included most of the city and began contracting its construction rather than using day laborers of its own. By 1920 city businesses and most of the city residences were connected to city sewer lines which conveyed the raw sewage to the Big Sioux River. Not until 1927, when the city had thirty thousand residents, did Sioux Falls construct its first sewage treatment plant.

The Big Sioux River and its environs provided Sioux Falls with outdoor recreational areas from the outset of the town's existence. In particular the heavily-wooded island just above the falls and adjacent to the downtown area long served as a community park. Privately owned by A. G. Seney, builder of the Queen Bee Mill, and known as Seney's Island or simply "the island," it was the community picnic ground and where celebrations like the Fourth of July were held. By the turn of the century, however, pollution of the river by city sewage and the press of rail yards with noisy and smelly locomotives had ruined its pastoral atmosphere. The end came in 1907 when the Sioux Falls Light and Power Company raised the level of the old Queen Bee millpond by sealing off the channel around the island. A few years later the Milwaukee Railroad Company purchased the island from Seney, filled in the channel, and cleared the trees to expand its freight yards.

The river itself provided the city recreational activities during its early decades. The Cascade Mill Dam just north of Eighth Street, constructed in 1878, raised and broadened the river through the downtown area and upstream beyond Twenty-sixth Street where two small islands split the current. One of these islands, "second island," was a popular picnic spot at the turn of the century, and one could get there by renting a small row boat or riding a steam launch from the foot of Ninth Street. In the winter the river served as the community ice skating rink, and in summer it was the municipal swimming pool. In the new century, however, pollution gradually discouraged recreational use of the river.

After 1900, as the city's residential neighborhoods moved further from the downtown segment of the river and as that part of the river became increasingly polluted, new recreational areas were established. In 1906, Mrs. Helen G. McKennan, sister of early settler Artemas Gale, gave 20 acres of land on the bluff south of downtown to the city to be developed as a city park. Four years later, E. A. Sherman donated to Sioux Falls 53 acres on the river southwest of the city for a second park. (In 1929 the city purchased an additional 152 acres to expand Sherman Park northward to Twelfth Street.) The area Sherman gave to the city had long been used as a picnic area, but after 1919 the city, under Sherman's personal direction, began developing the site into the community's new river recreation site. In 1916 the city purchased 20 acres at Covell Lake from the Phillips estate to create a third major park.

This period of the city's history, 1898 to 1918, began and ended with a war. The Spanish-American War that occurred during three months in the spring of 1898 had major consequences for the nation but few for Sioux Falls. World War I, however, was a different matter. For nearly three years after war broke out in Europe in 1914 the United States was officially neutral, but Sioux Falls participated in the emotional events that led to its entrance on the side of the allies. Once the United States was in the war, the city participated in the all-out war effort orchestrated by

Jewett Brothers and Jewett Wholesale Grocers built this new warehouse facility at Fifth and Phillips in 1899. They had been in the Blauvelt Building at Fifth and Main since coming to town in 1890. When the Jewetts retired from business in 1927 the building was sold to Nash Finch Wholesale Grocers. It is currently occupied by Lindsay Brothers. Center for Western Studies photo

the Wilson administration. City residents assisted nearby farmers with harvests to compensate for the farm laborers who were now in the military. Victory gardens were planted, and scrap metal and War Bond drives became regular events. State authorized agencies made sure that everyone fully supported the war effort.

The war that began when Congress declared hostilities against Germany in April, 1917, had a lasting effect on Sioux Falls and its people. Sioux Falls became caught up in an intense orchestrated war effort to make sure everyone was a 100 percent loyal American. To be a hyphenated American was not enough, and German-Americans, who had been valued and respected citizens, were suddenly viewed with suspicion. An anti-German movement occurred during 1917 and 1918 that destroyed the German-American Alliance, an organization to celebrate the German ethnic heritage; closed down the German language newspaper, the *Deutscher Herold*, and arrested its editor for treason under the Espionage Act; prohibited the teaching of foreign languages in the public schools; and made it illegal to speak German in public when more than three people were gathered. World War I effectively destroyed the ethnic cohesiveness of German-Americans, and it has never been reestablished.

The war hysteria did not confine its energies only to German-Americans. Former United States Senator R. F. Pettigrew was charged with treason under the war Espionage Act for stating to an *Argus Leader* reporter his opposition to the declaration of war as a move to promote the financial interests of American munitions manufacturers. On the night of April 3, 1918, the "Yellow Paint Brigade" painted the word

Beware in large yellow letters on Pettigrew's office door and on the doors of homes and businesses of others who were suspected of being pro-German. Windows were broken and in several cases serious vandalism occurred. Apparent illness postponed Pettigrew's being brought to trial prior to the end of the war, and the charges were ultimately dropped.

The war also had a lasting effect on the city's economy. Wartime demand for goods raised wages and prices, and the community shared in the wartime prosperity. Not all segments of the community shared equally, however. The quarry industry, for instance, never recovered from the shortage of railroad cars caused by war mobilization. On the other hand, the shortage of railroad cars to transport livestock to the Sioux Falls stockyard led many farmers to purchase trucks for hauling their animals to market. Wholesale distributors, too, began turning to trucks to transport their goods to regional retailers. Railroads, as a result, became less crucial to the economic welfare of Sioux Falls as a result of the war.

During the first two decades of the twentieth century Sioux Falls harvested the fruits of its founders' labors in making the city a regional railroad center. Its rail connections to the surrounding market area made it a natural distributing center for wholesalers and small manufacturers. The rapid expansion of these activities after 1900 attracted people seeking jobs and they in turn stimulated the growth of the city's retail trade. The irony of the period is that during this high point of the railroad's influence on the city's well-being, Sioux Falls entered the automobile era. In the next decades the city's boosters would become more interested in roads than railroads.

The newly-established professional fire department at its headquarters in the City Auditorium Building. Horses would not be replaced with motor vehicles until 1917. Center for Western Studies photo

The Carnegie Library, completed in 1903, was made possible by a twenty-five thousand dollar gift from steel millionaire Andrew Carnegie. Various attempts had been made since 1875 to establish a permanent library in Sioux Falls, but none were successful until W. H. Lyon gave the city the abandoned Unitarian Church Building for that purpose in 1899. Soon after moving to the new location, news came of Carnegie's offer. The city decided it should accept the gift and Mr. and Mrs. Lyon agreed. Center for Western Studies photo

William H. Lyon, born at Carrol, Iowa in 1858, came to Sioux Falls in the fall of 1883 after completing law school. He was well-educated, a successful lawyer and, along with his wife, Winona, a generous supporter of the community's development. Center for Western Studies photo

The new Andrew Kuehn Wholesale Grocery building at Sixth and Phillips in 1900. It was one of many warehouses built north of Sixth Street at the turn of the century to serve an expanded wholesale trade area in the region. This handsome quartzite building has been refurbished and is now an apartment building with a commercial area on the ground floor. Center for Western Studies photo

The Sioux Falls Malting Works is shown here upon completion in 1902. This new company, a spin-off of the brewery, produced malt for other breweries in the Midwest and as far away as the Pacific Coast. Center for Western Studies photo

The Lutheran Normal School is pictured here in 1905 upon completion of Ladies Hall, now known as East Hall. It became Augustana College in 1918 when Augustana moved from Canton, South Dakota, and merged with the Sioux Falls school that had been founded in 1889. At this time cornfields surrounded the campus as the southern edge of the city was about at Twenty-second Street. Center for Western Studies photo

The Manchester Biscuit Company Building and its employees were photographed shortly after the building was completed in 1902. Local wholesale grocers, Andrew Kuehn and Jewett Brothers and Jewett convinced L. D. Manchester to move his bakery from Luverne, Minnesota to Sioux Falls in 1902. Beginning with this modest two story building the business grew steadily through the years requiring additions to the building on a regular basis, the last in 1946. The United Biscuit Company of America owned the plant in 1960 when production was discontinued in Sioux Falls. Since 1961 the Manchester Building has been occupied by Raven Industries. Center for Western Studies photo

The new Sioux Falls Brewery was constructed in 1904. The Sioux Falls Brewery, begun in 1875, was one of the city's most successful industries. It was hampered, but not closed by state prohibition from 1890 to 1896 and this handsome building is good evidence of its success after 1898. It was closed by the passage of National Prohibition in 1919. Center for Western Studies photo

This photo was taken looking north from the court-house tower in about 1905. This area, the main wholesale district, developed after 1899 as railroads made the city the main wholesale distribution center of the surrounding region. The Standard Oil Company's tanks can be seen in the center of the photo. Center for Western Studies photo

This view looks south on Main Avenue from the court-house tower at Sixth in about 1905. The area between Sixth and Eighth was never as well-developed as the area south of Eighth, and served as a buffer zone between the retail and wholesale districts. Center for Western Studies photo

Note the City Auditorium in the upper left and First Baptist Church slightly below and to its right in this view looking southwest from the court-house tower in about 1905. The area west of Dakota is still mainly residential. Center for Western Studies photo

This view looks south on Phillips Avenue from Eighth Street in about 1905. In 1907 the new trolley was installed on Phillips, but little else would change in the block between Eighth and Ninth for several years. Center for Western Studies photo

The Manchester Biscuit Company is on the upper left and the Merchant Hotel is the white building in the lower center of this 1905 photo taken looking southeast from the court-house tower. Henry George Cigars was one of several brands made in Sioux Falls at the time. Center for Western Studies photo

GROCERIES CROCKERY

This 1904-05 picture of Main Avenue, looking north from Ninth Street, shows the Metropolitan Block, built in 1886, the location of the Minnehaha National Bank from 1887 to 1898. Next door to the north is the Ramsey Building built in 1890, and beyond that the Argus Leader Building. The Syndicate Block is at the end of the block and the County Court House can be seen in the distance. Main Avenue had been paved in 1892 from Third to Thirteenth Streets. Center for Western Studies photo

Looking east from the court-house tower in about 1905, this photo shows Jewett Brothers and Jewett Wholesale Grocers' building on the left. The wooded area is Seney Island. The Milwaukee freight depot is at the lower right. Center for Western Studies photo

The Paulton Block at Eleventh and Phillips was built in 1906 as a theater, but was never used for that purpose, being turned into offices and retail shops during construction. This is one of Wallace Dow's last designs before he died in 1911. The building was expanded to the south just before the time of this picture in about 1910. The photo is taken from the new Boyce-Greeley Building erected that year. Center for Western Studies photo

This view of Phillips Avenue south from Seventeenth Street in 1907 shows a new residential area of the time. In 1914 Phillips Avenue became the first residential street to be paved when pavement was extended to Twenty-first Street. Street paving of residential areas progressed steadily during the 1920s, and in the 1930s it continued with work relief funding from the federal government. Center for Western Studies photo

The Pressed Brick Company, established in 1903, was one of the several brickyards in Sioux Falls in the early years of this century. Brick largely replaced quartzite in the construction of business buildings after the depression of 1893 because of its cost advantage. Locally produced bricks, however, were often not the most durable because of the poor clay. Center for Western Studies photo

This 1907 picture shows the Sioux Falls Brewery and Malting Works on North Main Avenue. The Brewery on the left, built in 1904, produced several brands of beer that were popular in the region. The Malting Works on the right, built in 1902, supplied malt to breweries all over the Midwest. Both closed in 1919 because of National Prohibition. The malt works buildings burned in the early 1960s, but the brewery building still stands. Center for Western Studies photo

The Sioux Falls Gas Works is shown here in 1903. The plant had not suffered an explosion since 1897, and in 1905 the Argus Leader *called it "the popular supplier of fuel both for lights and for cooking." In 1906 the city failed to renew its contract with the gas company for street lighting. In 1931 a pipeline from Texas was completed to bring natural gas to the city. Center for Western Studies photo*

The Sioux Falls Broom Works was photographed in 1909. The Kuh brothers began this industry on the East side in 1887. On January 1, 1909 the Argus Leader reported that they were producing two hundred thousand brooms annually and employed sixteen people. Nick Ehlen photo

This 1907 postcard indicates that the new Sioux Falls Traction System had five miles of track and three cars. There were eventually five lines and many cars, but the increasing expense of laying tracks to outlying areas and increased automobile usage ended the trolley in 1929 when it was totally replaced by bus service. Center for Western Studies photo

This 1908 picture shows the Sioux Falls Light and Power Company's newly completed hydro-electric plant. It used three water turbines to generate electricity after raising and improving the Queen Bee's millpond and headworks. Steam driven generators were later added and the plant expanded as the city's consumption of electricity increased. Water power was used for backup until World War II. Center for Western Studies photo

The Pankow Brothers Foundry, located at Second and Eleventh, operated in Sioux Falls from 1884 to 1926. The cast iron used in many buildings constructed in Sioux Falls, including the Old Court House, was made in their shop. This picture shows the foundry as it looked about 1905. Center for Western Studies photo

The five Pankow brothers are pictured here. Center for Western Studies photo

This interior shot shows the Pankow Brothers Foundry. The five Pankow brothers produced many of the city's manhole covers, coal chutes, and other iron goods until their retirement in 1926. Center for Western Studies photo

Ninth and Dakota was photographed looking east after the blizzard of February 6, 1909. In the old days there were no snowblowers or street snowplows. Heavy snow brought the city to a standstill for days as the snow was shoveled on wagons and hauled to the river. The City Auditorium is on the left. Center for Western Studies photo

The launch Cecil is shown here on the Big Sioux River near Second Island around the turn of the century. Excursions from the Ninth Street Dock to the picnic islands upstream on this steam-powered vessel were quite popular in the early years of this century. Center for Western Studies photo

This photo of the Northwestern Telephone Exchange Company was taken around the turn of the century. Sioux Falls received telephone service very early, with the first system installed in 1882 with a capital of ten thousand dollars and thirty subscribers. This company merged with Northwestern Bell in 1921. Sioux Falls 1956 Centennial Souvenir Program photo

A
HOME
INSTITUTION

A TELEPHONE

IN YOUR RESIDENCE, $1.25 PER MONTH
IN YOUR OFFICE, :: $1.50 PER MONTH

1,700

SUBSCRIBERS IN SIOUX FALLS AND SURROUNDING COUNTRY :: :: ::

SIOUX FALLS PEOPLE HAVE OVER $90,000.00 INVESTED :: :: :: ::

Citizens Telephone Company

In 1900 the Citizens Telephone Company was organized to compete with the Northwestern Telephone and Exchange Company. This 1905 advertisement shows how rapidly the company had grown, but in 1908 Citizens sold out to the New State Telephone Company, which in 1919 sold to the Iowa Telephone Company. In 1921 this company also merged with Bell Telephone. Center for Western Studies photo

This view of Phillips Avenue looks north from Tenth Street in 1908. The trolley electric poles are a new obstruction in the street, but probably caused no serious traffic problem since there were as yet few automobiles. That would change in a very short time. Center for Western Studies photo

Looking north from the roof of the new Washington High School Building in 1907-08, this photo shows the new Masonic Temple, constructed in 1905, on the far left. On the far right is the L. D. Miller Livery Barn. The L. D. Miller Undertaking Building, predecessor to the current Miller Funeral Home, is just north of the barn. Center for Western Studies photo

The Congregational Church, built in 1909, replaced the original frame church on the same site at Eleventh and Dakota. It was the last church in Sioux Falls to be built of quartzite, and the first of several "second generation" church buildings erected in the first two decades of the twentieth century. Center for Western Studies photo

City Temple Baptist Church was built in 1910 at the corner of Eighth and Spring to replace the congregation's original frame church built in 1878 at Eighth and Dakota. In 1951 the congregation moved again to the current First Baptist Church on Twenty-second and Covell Avenue. Center for Western Studies photo

First Presbyterian Church was constructed in 1914 at Tenth and Spring. The congregation was first organized in 1883 and built its first building two years later at Tenth and Minnesota. Nearly thirty years later the congregation's continued growth required a new, larger church. In 1956 the congregation moved again to its present building at Thirtieth and West Avenue and sold this one to the Seventh Day Adventists. Center for Western Studies photo

Rush Brown of the Brown Drug Company was photographed in his new Fawick Flyer. Thomas Fawick designed and assembled five of these three-thousand-dollar automobiles in Sioux Falls between 1908 and 1910. This particular one is reputedly the first four-door car ever made. Center for Western Studies photo

Theodore Roosevelt Day was celebrated in Sioux Falls. In the fall of 1910 former President Roosevelt came to Sioux Falls, and is seen here standing in the back seat of Rush Brown's Fawick Flyer during a parade on Phillips Avenue. Center for Western Studies photo

The new Central Fire Station was built in 1912 at Ninth and Minnesota after the fire department had outgrown its quarters in the City Auditorium. The old fire bell was moved, along with the department, and mounted in the new building's handsome tower. Center for Western Studies photo

The first airplane came to Sioux Falls on a railroad flatcar in 1912 to put on a flying show at Coat's Field, a popular race track near present-day east Twenty-Sixth Street and the river. Airplanes were rare in Sioux Falls until 1929 when an airfield was laid out on the site of the present-day Western Mall on Forty-first Street. Center for Western Studies photo

The original spillway near the Penitentiary was completed in 1908. This was the first real attempt at controlling spring floods on the Big Sioux by constructing a drainage ditch and spillway that carried excess water from north of the city directly to the river below the downtown area. It provided a shortcut for the river that avoided the downtown. A major flood in 1915 destroyed this spillway, and the city and the farmers north of the city argued for years over who should pay the cost of its replacement. The two parties finally agreed to share the cost, but the flood system was not perfected until the late 1950s. Center for Western Studies photo

The new Eighth Street Bridge is shown here just after its completion in 1912. The old Cascade Mill Dam in the foreground was removed in 1959 as part of the Army Corps of Engineers's flood control project in the downtown area. Center for Western Studies photo

A road crew with horses and scrapers built Highway 77 between Sioux Falls and Dell Rapids in 1913. To travel to Sioux Falls by any means other than the railroad was hazardous, and in some seasons impossible in the early decades of this century. Few South Dakota roads were graded and none were graveled prior to 1920. Highway 77 to Dell Rapids was the first paved highway in the state when it was completed in 1932. Siouxland Heritage Museums photo

The R. F. Pettigrew family lived at Eighth and Duluth. Pettigrew purchased this house, designed by W. L. Dow and built in 1889, when he returned to Sioux Falls in 1912 after twenty years absence. In the 1890s he had been in Washington, D.C., as South Dakota's senator. After failing to be reelected in 1900, he moved to New York City where he lived while he rebuilt the fortune he had lost in the panic of 1893. He constructed an addition to the house in 1925 in which to display his personal museum collection. In 1926, when he died, the house and his collections were given to Sioux Falls for a museum. Siouxland Heritage Museums photo

In 1911 the United Flour Milling Company of Minneapolis purchased the Queen Bee Mill after it had stood idle for nearly thirty years. The new owners converted the mill to electric power and operated it until 1916. It was reopened by the Larabee Flour Company in 1917 and closed for the final time shortly after World War I. Siouxland Heritage Museums photo

99

This early 1912 picture of the John Morrell Plant was taken from the Queen Bee Mill. The old Green Packing Plant, originally built in 1891 as a linen mill, and where Morrell's started when it came to town in 1909, is next to the river at the center of the picture. Center for Western Studies photo

In 1916 the Wisconsin Granite Company quarry was located just south of the present-day stockyards. By this time quartzite was being used almost totally for paving and for lining steel furances. This quarry was abandoned in 1918 and a new one started on West Madison Street. Siouxland Heritage Museums photo

The original McKennan Hospital opened in 1911. Helen McKennan left a gift of twenty-five thousand dollars in her will for starting a hospital in Sioux Falls. The gift was not sufficient by itself, but through Bishop O'Gorman's leadership additional money was raised to build the hospital, and the Presentation Sisters from Aberdeen agreed to manage and staff it. Center for Western Studies photo

Dr. Harry Subera, long-time Sioux Falls doctor, was photographed in his office, a typical physician's office of the early twentieth century. Siouxland Heritage Museums photo

The Munce Brothers Moving Company's fleet of horses and moving vans is shown here at Fourth and Indiana in 1912.

Trucks began replacing horses and wagons during World War I, but some delivery services like milk companies continued to

use horses as late as 1952 because they could be taught the route and know where to stop. Munce Brothers photo

This is the interior of the Sugar Bowl, a popular restaurant at 105 South Phillips Avenue in the teens and early twenties. Siouxland Heritage Museums photo

Look's Meat Market was located at Eighth and Main in the early years of this century. In the days before refrigeration, people shopped for fresh meat on a daily basis. Note the home-made bologna on the counter, one of the few cooked meats available at the store in this period. Siouxland Heritage Museums photo

This view shows the west side of Phillips Avenue between Eleventh and Tenth streets in 1912. On the right is the just-completed Carpenter Hotel which boasted of being "fire-proof," a quality that was more significant to Sioux Falls after the Cataract Hotel fire in 1900 and the Merchant's Hotel fire in 1912. On the left is the Boyce-Greeley Building, constructed in 1910 by local lawyer Jesse Boyce and George Greeley, a real estate man. The building is unique because it is actually two separate but identical buildings constructed by two different contractors but sharing a common entrance. Siouxland Heritage Museums photo

Boating was popular in Sherman Park about 1915. In 1910 E. A. Sherman, long time businessman in Sioux Falls, gave the city fifty-three acres of land along the river for a park. The city constructed retaining walls and a dam on the river to raise the water level for swimming and boating. In the late twenties or early thirties the city built cabins in the park to house motoring tourists. Center for Western Studies photo

Edwin A. Sherman, born in Massachusetts in 1844, came to Sioux Falls in 1873 and began a long and active career in business and civic affairs. He served as county superintendent of schools from 1874 to 1886 when most of the county schools were organized, constructed a large number of business buildings, platted Sherman's Addition, built the Cascade Flour Mill in 1878 and added the city's first electric generating plant to it in 1887, served on the first city commission in 1908, and donated the land to create the public park that bears his name. Photo from George Kingsbury's History of Dakota Territory, Vol. IV

The McKennan Park Pool is shown here in about 1917. As the city expanded further from the river, and as the river became more polluted after 1900, new parks were established. In 1906 Mrs. Helen G. McKennan gave twenty acres of land to the city for a park at Twenty-first Street and Second Avenue, which was then the edge of town. Siouxland Heritage Museums photo

Helen McKennan, sister of Artemas Gale, created the city's first public park when she gave her home and the land surrounding it to the city for that purpose upon her death in 1906. She also provided the seed money for the creation of McKennan Hospital. Photo from Charles A. Smith's Minnehaha County History

This photo looks west on Tenth Street from Phillips Avenue in 1916. The F. W. Woolworth Store had just moved into the old C. K. Howard Building on the corner, and next to it on Tenth is the Egyptian Theatre, one of the city's first movie theatres, built in 1913. Horses would be a common sight on Sioux Falls streets until after World War I. Center for Western Studies photo

The East Side Fire Station and Library Building in 1917 were photographed when the adjacent Library Park was being completed. The fire house was built to provide better fire protection to the growing East Side. In 1917 the city bought the remainder of the block at Weber and Sixth, a former quarry site, from R. F. Pettigrew and developed a park and wading pool. The Sioux Falls Park Department's offices now occupy the building. Center for Western Studies photo

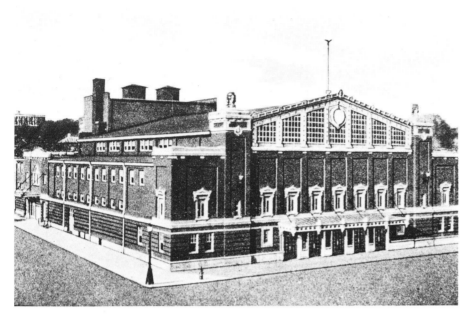

The City Coliseum at Fifth and Main, constructed in 1917 at a cost of $120,000, was intended to replace the City Auditorium as the public auditorium and convention center. It originally had portable seating that could be removed for dances, dinners, sporting events and exhibits. Pres. Woodrow Wilson spoke here in 1919 as he toured the country seeking to convince Americans their country should join his League of Nations. In 1932 a large annex was constructed to provide better facilities for conventions and basketball games. The Annex burned in 1973. Center for Western Studies photo

Dickenson's Blacksmith Shop, located in the old First Methodist Church Building at Eleventh and Main, is shown here in about 1915. His signs says "machinery of all kinds repaired," and that now included automobiles. Blacksmiths, too, had to adjust to the new auto age. The first wing of Washington High School, completed in 1907, is on the right. Center for Western Studies photo

The Argus Leader *Building on the west side of Main just north of Ninth is pictured here sometime after it added a second story in 1917. The electric bulletin board printed out the latest news received over the wire services. In the days before radio, crowds gathered in the street to learn the outcome of elections and baseball games. This building was destroyed by fire in 1951. Center for Western Studies photo*

The Moe Hospital at Fourteenth and Main was built in 1917 by Doctor Anton Moe. It continued to operate as a private hospital and clinic until 1941. The building stood vacant until 1942 when it was converted into an office building. Center for Western Studies photo

St. Joseph Cathedral, constructed between 1915 and 1918, replaced the earlier Catholic Cathedral of St. Michael's that had stood at that location since 1883. Nearby Cathedral School was founded in 1915 with its present building being erected in 1926. Center for Western Studies photo

This view shows Phillips Avenue looking south from Eighth Street in about 1917. This block remained nearly unchanged until urban renewal began in the 1960s. Center for Western Studies photo

Phillips Avenue was photographed looking south from Ninth Street in about 1916-17. The Edmison-Jamison Building, later known as the Minnehaha Building, is on the right, and the next tall one is the Bee Hive Department Store. The Bee Hive, established in 1893, moved into this bulding in 1901 and continued there until 1935 when Montgomery Ward's became its new tenant. Note all the awnings along the street to keep the morning sun's heat out of the unairconditioned buildings. City Traffic Department photo

Looking north on Phillips Avenue from the Paulton Block in about 1916-17, one can see that automobiles were rapidly taking over the streets of the city, as there are only a few horses in this picture. Center for Western Studies photo

Looking north on Phillips from Twelfth Street in 1917, this view shows the preponderance of large buildings on the west side of the street, but construction of the Shriver-Johnson Department Store building the next year would help redress the imbalance. Sioux Falls Traffic Department photo

The Fantle Brothers Department Store was photographed the morning after the fire which destroyed the three-year-old building in February 1918. Fantles rebuilt in the same location (the west side of Phillips and south of Ninth), and remained there until 1939 when they moved to their new building at Ninth and Main. J. C. Penney's occupied the old Fantle Building on Phillips until it moved to the Empire Mall in 1975. Center for Western Studies photo

This view shows the west side of Minnesota Avenue just north of Eighteenth Street in the late teens. Peterson's Fancy Groceries on the left was typical of the many small corner grocery stores that sprang up in residential neighborhoods after the turn of the century. The rapid growth of the city after 1900 made it increasingly inconvenient for people to get downtown for shopping. The corner grocery served the walking distance neighborhood women who needed to shop almost daily for perishable foods. Center for Western Studies photo

*Service Day was celebrated in Sioux Falls
on May 21, 1919. The city turned out to
cheer and welcome home the soldiers who
had returned from serving in what President Wilson said was to be the war to end
all wars. The sign on the arch reads
"Sioux Falls Honors and Welcomes All
Who Have Served." Center for Western
Studies photo*

From Rails to Roads 1918 to 1940

Transportation continued to be the key to Sioux Falls's growth and prosperity in the two decades after 1920, as it had been since the city was founded. Prior to 1920 the railroads had been the source of the thriving wholesale, retail and manufacturing trade that had made Sioux Falls grow and prosper. City fathers had worked hard and the community had provided the necessary money to insure its acquisition of the all-important rail connections to eastern markets and to the smaller communities of the surrounding region. In the 1920s Sioux Falls promoters worked equally hard and put up the necessary money to make sure the city acquired the highway connections that would enable the city to continue its growth and prosperity in the auto age.

The booster spirit was still very much alive in Sioux Falls in the 1920s. In 1924, the *Sioux Falls Journal* printed "Know and Grow with Sioux Falls and South Dakota," a chamber of commerce promotion booklet, aimed at making Sioux Falls a city of fifty thousand people by 1930. The booklet included the usual brief history of the city and numerous articles on successful businesses and businessmen, and the assets that the city had to offer prospective residents and investors. But where earlier promotional literature focused on railroads, this 1924 piece devoted a great deal of space to the topic of roads and highways. "Good roads," wrote the chamber secretary, "are working a revolution in both trade and social life. A graveled or hard-surfaced road," he explained, "is a continued invitation and the open door to neighborliness. The fine graveled roads extending out for several hours' fast driving in all directions from Sioux Falls," he stated, "have increased its retail territory greatly and

The Preparedness Parade was photographed marching north on Phillips Avenue in the spring of 1917 as Sioux Falls prepared a send-off for its young men headed for World War I in France. The photo shows the east side of Phillips between Eleventh and Twelfth. Siouxland Heritage Museums photo

The Home Guard drilled at the athletic field east of the present day Nelson Field during World War I. The pictured athletic field was constructed by the school district in 1916, and in 1939 it was named Howard Wood Field in honor of the man who coached at Washington High School from 1910 to 1943. In the distance toward the right is the Children's Home, current site of Lewis Drug Eastgate. Center for Western Studies photo

The Hudson, Essex Agency was built in 1919 at Ninth and Dakota, the center of the auto district in Sioux Falls. Most of the city's auto dealers were within one block of this intersection. The automobile brought fundamental changes to Sioux Falls and the lives of its residents. Center for Western Studies photo

this will continue for some time." Good roads also added to the wholesale business of the city. The chamber secretary reported that twenty-seven truck lines were then operating between Sioux Falls and other towns. "The city and the village alike," he concluded, "must adjust themselves to meet the new situations." He might have included the railroads, for by 1928 they began the process of abandoning depots in small towns.

Roads involved more than sustaining and increasing Sioux Falls's regional leadership as a wholesale, retail and manufacturing center. Local business leaders had discovered the tourist. U.S.G. Cherry, a local attorney, authored an article in the 1924 promotional booklet describing the efforts of "the business interests of the city" to create the Atlantic, Yellowstone and Pacific Highway which he termed "the main street of the United States." It was crucial for Sioux Falls to make sure that a transcontinental highway passed through the city, for, as he put it, "it is now recognized that the largest crop in every state is the tourist traffic, during the tourist season."

Cherry proceeded to describe how a year earlier Sioux Falls businessmen had incorporated a foundation and raised thirty-five thousand dollars to promote the development of this transcontinental highway that would bring tourist traffic to their city. They had solicited the cooperation of cities and towns along the route and set up highway markers eastward to Waterloo, Iowa, a distance of 316 miles. Nearly the entire distance consisted of graveled or paved roads, and from Waterloo there was a good highway to Chicago. Since the state of South Dakota was constructing a graveled road from Sioux Falls to Rapid City, Sioux Falls would be on a major highway from the East that would carry tourists to the Badlands, the Black Hills, Yellowstone and even the Pacific Coast. Here was the origin of Highway 16 and Interstate 90. Sioux Falls had never acquired a transcontinental railroad, but it did acquire a transcontinental highway.

South Dakota had few graded roads before 1915 and by 1920 none were yet graveled. Local chamber-of-commerce organizations and automobile owners pushed for road improvement, but it was federal money that made it happen. South Dakota created a state highway department in 1917 to qualify for federal road building funds under the Federal Highway Act of 1916. This federal money plus revenues from license fees and gasoline taxes enabled the state to launch an ambitious road building program in the 1920s. The legislature had determined that roads should be built linking the state's major cities together in a grid of north, south and east, west routes. Sioux Falls became a junction on this grid of new highways. The first concrete highway in the state, between Sioux Falls and Dell Rapids, was not completed until 1932.

The trolley, too, lost out to the motor vehicle as city streets were rapidly extended and paved during the 1920s. Trolley lines had not kept pace with the rapid expansion of the city's residential areas after 1915, and in 1922 the first motor buses appeared on Sioux Falls's streets. In 1929, after the death of its founder Frank Moody Mills, the trolley company ceased operations. City taxpayers constructed paved streets for buses, and trolley lines that had to build and maintain their own rail systems could not compete. Cost and flexibility were the determining factors.

The impact of the automobile upon Sioux Falls increased as their numbers increased. During the war there was a rapid growth in the number of trucks used by businessmen to deliver goods to customers. By the early twenties almost all city deliveries except coal, ice and milk were being made using motorized vehicles. Horse-drawn milk-delivery wagons persisted until the early 1950s because of their convenience to the milkman. It was never possible to teach a truck to follow down the street, stopping at the right places, while the milkman ran up to the houses with the milk.

Long-established businesses were forever changed or destroyed by the passing of the horse as the dominant means of transportation. The livery barn that cared for and rented horses and rigs gradually disappeared from Sioux Falls with the last one closing in about 1921. (The modern car-rental agency would be a rough equivalent.) And, the blacksmith shop either converted to repairing automobiles and became a garage or went out of business. A new institution, the gas station, became the fastest growing business of the twenties and thirties, and the horse trader was replaced by the used car salesman.

The automobile improved the atmosphere of Sioux Falls—its smell if not its noise level. The tons of horse manure and oceans of urine that had graced city streets and attracted flies, as well as the backyard barns and manure piles in residential neighborhoods were gone by the end of the 1920s.

In 1920 business leaders in Sioux Falls expected that the prosperous boom times of the previous decade

This shows Phillips Avenue north from Seventh Street in about 1918. The Orpheum on the left was erected in 1913 as a vaudeville stage theater but also had a projector to show movies between acts. Little did they know how quickly the motion picture would replace the live acts and change the theater business. In the center is the Albert Hotel which replaced the Merchants Hotel after it burned in 1912. Center for Western Studies photo

would continue. The new auto age was in full bloom in 1920. Sioux Falls car dealers, operating out of large, new buildings, sold cars faster than they could get them from the factory. Implement wholesalers and retailers were doing a brisk business selling new tractor powered farm equipment, and electric home appliances were gaining popularity.

But in 1921 the artificial boom of the war years ended. Overproduction soon caused a drop in agricultural prices and with it came a drop in the value of farm land. Farmers, who had borrowed money to buy expensive land or new equipment during the war boom, soon found themselves unable to repay their loans. In 1921 one state bank in South Dakota failed; by January of 1925 the number totaled 175.

Sioux Falls shared in the misfortunes of the surrounding countryside in the 1920s. But before deflation began in 1921, several important building projects were completed that had been postponed by the war effort including the new YMCA, Columbus College, an addition to Washington High School, the Augustana College Administration Building, and the Sioux Falls Medical and Surgical Clinic. After 1921 Sioux Falls experienced its share of bank and business failures, but the population continued to grow and a surprising number of buildings were constructed. In fact, by 1929, Sioux Falls was in the midst of a building-and-business boom that was cut short by the stock market crash in October.

The Great Depression that began with the stock market crash had a dramatic impact on the Sioux Falls economy. In the month of October 1929 building permits valued at over two million dollars were issued. Two years later less than that amount was issued during the entire year, and in 1933—the depression's

low point—only a quarter of a million dollars of new construction occurred in the city. In the remainder of the 1930s major construction consisted primarily of public works projects sponsored by the city or county under the Public Works Administration and Works Progress Administration of the Roosevelt New Deal. PWA and WPA projects included Lowell School addition in 1935, the new City Hall and the final wing of Washington High School in 1936, the new Irving School, the National Guard Armory, and the County Court House Annex in 1937, and the Municipal Airport in 1938-1939. Throughout the New Deal period, the construction and paving of city streets continued with federal employment-relief funding.

Sioux Falls began to recover slowly from the Depression after 1935. The population, which remained stagnant from 1930 to 1935, began to grow again, and by 1940 seven thousand residents had been added to the census total. Construction of new homes, which had reached a low of only fifty in 1934, gradually increased in succeeding years to accommodate the growing population. In 1938 two major business construction projects were announced. L. D. Miller replaced the old Commercial House/Teton Hotel with a combination store and theater building (Hollywood), and Ben Fantle constructed a new two story store building on the site of the old YMCA block at Ninth and Main.

The Sioux Falls Chamber of Commerce worked vigorously to make Sioux Falls a convention city during the 1920s and 1930s, and they were generally successful. The city Coliseum, constructed in 1917, was the city's primary convention facility, but it was soon inadequate and in 1932 the city constructed an annex that tripled its floor space. The chamber of

commerce convention section billed Sioux Falls as "the Meeting Place for the Northwest," and promoted the city's convention business throughout the region. In the year previous to July 1, 1938, the city hosted over sixty large conventions (the largest being the annual meeting of the South Dakota Education Association) and about four hundred sales meetings. But the chamber felt it was the logical location to host even larger, regional conventions. *An Economic and Social Survey of Sioux Falls*, compiled in 1938, stated that what the city needed to become a major convention center was a "first class hotel." It had three major hotels and six others, but their capacity did not match that of the Coliseum and none had adequate convention facilities of its own. The desire to be a major regional convention center is an old and enduring Sioux Falls tradition.

Sioux Falls also entered the air age in the period after 1920. Prior to World War I, the airplane was an item of curiosity. The first one arrived on a railroad flat car for an exhibition in 1912, but by 1921 an air circus flew into town and in 1929 a private airport was established in the area south of Forty-first Street and west of Western Avenue. The chamber of commerce sponsored air shows in the late 1920s to stimulate interest in aviation, and in 1932 airmail service began in Sioux Falls. The Depression of the early 1930s, however, postponed further development of commercial aviation in the city.

As commercial aviation matured in the 1930s, Sioux Falls again worked to make sure it retained its position as a transportation center. The Federal Air Mail Act of 1934 began the process of establishing routes for commercial airlines, and by 1938 the initial shake-out period was past. Federal air mail contracts subsidized the development of commercial aviation just as mail contracts had subsidized railroad operations in the past. By 1937 Sioux Falls knew it would need good airport facilities to secure a place on a commercial air route. Consequently, in 1937 Sioux Falls purchased land north of the city for a municipal airport. With WPA funding, runways and buildings were constructed, and in 1939 Mid-Continent Airlines began providing Sioux Falls with regular twice-daily airmail and passenger service.

It is interesting to note how quickly new technological innovations were introduced in Sioux Falls. This was true for telephones and electric lighting in the 1880s, and it was true of radio in the 1920s. The first commercial radio station was established in Pittsburg, Pennsylvania, in 1921, and the next year station WFAT, owned by the *Argus Leader,* began broadcasting from the top floor of the Carpenter Hotel. Charles Norton, WFAT manager and everything else, later recalled that the station "broadcast music, weather reports and market reports during the day and at night a musical program when we could scrape up free talent." (Smith, 176) In 1926 Joseph Henkin purchased the station and equipment, organized the Sioux Falls Broadcasting Company, and began operating the station as KSOO. Its studios were in the Manchester Biscuit Company building until the fall of 1937 when it moved to 317 South Phillips Avenue. By 1937 the radio business had developed sufficiently to warrant Henkin creating a second station, KELO. The Federal Communication Commission, frowning on one person owning two stations in the community, forced Henkin to sell one of his stations in 1946, and Sam Fantle, Jr., the purchaser, formed the Mid-continent Broadcasting Company to operate it.

The new YMCA Building at Eleventh and Minnesota was completed in 1921. The war delayed construction of this four hundred thousand dollar building, and it was the culmination of community efforts to revive the organization that had been dormant since the 1890s. The YWCA was organized in 1921, but its building was not erected until 1936. Center for Western Studies photo

The Crescent Creamery moved into the Brewery Building on north Main after National Prohibition closed it in 1919. The Crescent Creamery was an established business when this photo was taken in the early 1920s, having been founded in 1912. Horses were used for milk delivery in Sioux Falls until the early 1950s. Photo from the Sioux Falls Centennial (1856-1956) Souvenir Program, 1956

The Twenty-first Street Boulevard is shown here in the early twenties when this area along McKennan Park was the southern edge of the city. Center for Western Studies photo

116

(Smith, 177).

In an age when electronic communication is taken for granted, it is difficult to understand the impact the radio had upon Sioux Falls and the surrounding region. It provided entertainment, of course, but more importantly it connected individual homes with national, state and local happenings. People for the first time were able to hear distant events as they occurred from presidential inaugurations to baseball games. Especially important to area farmers were the market reports. For the first time they knew what farm prices were before they loaded up and headed for town. For Sioux Falls, the enterprise of Norton, Henkin and Fantle meant that it would become a regional communication center as well as a transportation center.

The rapid improvement in roads and automobiles in the 1920s and 1930s had negative as well as positive consequences. For one thing, it meant that criminals were more mobile and more difficult to catch. To counter this new criminal mobility, the Sioux Falls Police Department began using automobiles in 1922 and installed bulky and undependable one-way radios in patrol cars in 1935. They could also call upon the FBI, expanded and revitalized by J. Edgar Hoover who became director in 1924, to help apprehend criminals who crossed state boundaries.

Sioux Falls experienced two spectacular crimes in the 1930s: the Security Bank holdup in 1934 and the powderhouse explosion and murder on the last day of 1936. The first of these, the so-called Dillinger holdup, began about 10:00 A.M. on March 6, 1934, when a big Packard car containing six men pulled up to the Security Bank at the southwest corner of Main and Ninth. Four of the men, dressed in long overcoats with the collars up and wearing hats pulled low, entered the bank, drew guns, including at least one machine gun, and announced it was a holdup. A bank employee pushed the alarm button and a loud clanging alarm began to sound outside the building. By the time the robbers left, a crowd, estimated to number about one thousand people, had gathered near the bank to watch. Customers and employees were forced to line up facing the wall while one of the robbers put an estimated forty-six thousand dollars in cash from the vault into a sack. About this time another of the holdup men spotted motorcycle patrolman Hale Keith running from the north toward the bank. Jumping onto a desk he opened fire through the window glass and seriously wounded Keith with four shots. "I got one, I got one," the man reportedly shouted. The holdup men then herded employees and customers ahead of them out to their car and forced the teller, Leo Olson, and four women to stand on the car's running board to act as a shield against police gun fire. As the Packard getaway car started south on Main Avenue a policemen fired a single shot into the car's radiator, but after stopping briefly the criminals kept going. (*Argus Leader*, March 6, 1934)

Three police cars pursued the fleeing holdup men down Minnesota Avenue. At Forty-first Street the male hostage was released and the women taken inside the car. Two miles later they stopped, fired on their pursuers with machine guns and spread roofing nails on the road. A few miles further they abandoned their disabled car, taking another from a farmer, and released the women. Police pursuers lost their quarry, and airplanes were called in to search for the criminals' car without success. They were never apprehended.

No one has ever been able to verify that John Dillinger was really one of the men that held up the Security Bank. It was certainly a Dillinger-like holdup right down to the use of roofing nails on the road, and witnesses thought one of the men looked like Dillinger. But other evidence seems to indicate that Dillinger could not have been present. It does seem clear, however, that the young man who did the shooting was "Baby Face" Nelson, the famous Chicago gunman.

The second major criminal event of the 1930s in Sioux Falls was the powderhouse blast of December 31, 1936. This, too, involved interstate criminals using automobiles to conduct their illegal activities. At 9:45 P.M. an explosion suddenly shook the entire countryside. The blast, heard up to fifty miles away, broke more than twenty thousand dollars worth of window glass in Sioux Falls and broke windows in other nearby towns as far away as Dell Rapids. Four tons of blasting powder and one and one-half tons of dynamite had exploded at the Larson Hardware Powderhouse five miles southeast of town leaving a crater more than fifty feet across and twenty-five feet deep.

A large number of people rushed to the scene of the explosion to find the crater and, lying in a slight depression, a woman critically wounded from several gunshots. From this woman, who eventually recovered, authorities learned the story of what had happened. The woman, Helen Seilers of Sioux City, had convinced her boyfriend Harold Baker to quit the

This is an artist's rendering of a river bank improvement program proposed in 1922, which included a new civic building at the foot of Ninth Street. The severe postwar depression that hit the country at about that time, however, probably prevented the project from being undertaken. River improvement in the downtown area did not begin until the 1970s when the city implemented its River Greenway Project to develop the natural beauty of the river with parks and bike trails. The Sioux Falls National Bank in the picture was built in 1918, but the bank closed in 1924. The Western Bank currently occupies this building at Ninth and Phillips. Center for Western Studies photo

Phillips Avenue was photographed looking south from Ninth Street about 1922. The new Fantle Store, just south of the Bee Hive, had been built in 1918-19 to replace the old store that burned in February 1918. On the left is the E. C. Olson Clothing Store which did business at that location until 1974. Center for Western Studies photo

This view of the Minnehaha Country Club golf course looks southeast from the club house toward Kiwanis Avenue in the early 1920s. The golf club, formed in 1905 by C. E. McKinney, W. L. Baker, Howard Simpson, Allen Fellows, and Dr. John Donahoe, was originally located east of McKennan Park. At the outset a share cost one hundred dollars and the annual membership fee was thirty-five dollars. In 1914 the club moved to its present location. Center for Western Studies photo

This baseball game took place at McKennan Park about 1920. Baseball was first played in Sioux Falls in the summer of 1870 when a group from Vermillion played a government survey crew that included R. F. Pettigrew and those at the abandoned Fort Dakota waiting to claim a piece of the military reservation. In 1889 the Sioux Falls Canaries, a semi-professional team, was organized., The Canaries achieved their greatest popularity during the sports-crazy years of the early twenties, but they were revived in 1930 and remained active for more than two decades. Center for Western Studies photo

bank robber gang of which he was a member. The other members of this Sioux City gang had agreed he could leave after they finished one more robbery in Sioux Falls, and Baker and Seilers had agreed to go along. In reality, the trip to Sioux Falls was designed to eliminate Seilers and Baker. The two were taken to the isolated powderhouse where the other gang members shot each of them several times and then detonated the explosives to destroy the evidence of their murders. They succeeded with Baker. Only a single piece of his thumb was ever found, but Seilers had managed to crawl away from the powderhouse and take shelter in a slight depression in the ground before the blast occurred. The three murderers were eventually captured and convicted of their crime.

Twentieth-century technology brought many changes to Sioux Falls in the twenties and thirties. Automobiles, trucks, and buses supplanted the horse and buggy/wagon, the railroad and the trolley. Street building and paving became a never-ending process as the city continued to grow. The motion picture became a major form of entertainment, replacing in popularity live theater and amateur shows. Radio brought entertainment right into people's homes and provided them the latest news, weather and market information. New technology changed the domestic scene even further. By 1938 nearly all homes in Sioux Falls had electric lights, 80 percent used gas for cooking, and nearly one quarter had electric refrigerators rather than the old-fashioned ice box. (Econ./Social Survey, 168) Finally, aviation had its early commercial beginnings in this period, even though it would not be until after World War II that it matured as a major means of public transportation. Through all these changes local business and government leaders succeeded in maintaining Sioux Falls's position as a regional transportation, retailing and convention center. Despite the Depression, the city grew.

The Sioux Falls Fire Department in 1930 showed off their motorized equipment. Two, if not three, of the trucks were among the department's original motorized vehicles when it stopped using horses in 1917. The unit on the left is a 1915 Seagrave pumper which was in service until the 1960s when it was given to the park department. It is now at the Dennis the Menace Playground in Sherman Park. Center for Western Studies photo

A motorcycle race was photographed at Coat's Field in about 1920. This race track, located in the area north of Twenty-sixth Street and just west of the river, was first established by Clark Coats on his Riverside Farm in 1888. The state fair was held at this site in 1890 and 1891, and the track saw much activity from local race horse owners, especially trotters, before the age of the automobile. Center for Western Studies photo

The Ark, on the left, was a dance hall in the teens and the twenties built on the small island at the end of Ninth Street. Today the Municipal Parking Ramp covers the island. Center for Western Studies photo

McKennan Hospital is shown here as it looked after its expansion in 1918. Begun with a twenty-five thousand dollar bequest from Helen McKennan in 1911, the hospital gained an early reputation for having fine medical facilities. Center for Western Studies photo

Columbus College, a Catholic boy's school built in 1921, is seen here as it looked in the 1920s. The land and buildings were purchased by the federal government during World War II, and in 1949 it was named the Royal C. Johnson Veteran's Memorial Hospital. Center for Western Studies photo

This three hundred foot slide installed at Sherman Park in the teens extended from the Indian Mounds at the top of the bluff down to the river below. It provided high speed thrills for Sioux Falls park-goers, especially when riders sat on pieces of waxed paper from the bakery. The slide proved to be so dangerous that it was taken down in the spring of 1921. Center for Western Studies photo

The Sioux Falls Medical and Surgical Clinic was built on the southwest corner of Eleventh and Minnesota Avenue in 1920. It was the first doctor's building in the city, and existed at that location until 1965 when it was razed and a new clinic building, the Donahoe, was erected on Minnesota Avenue between Twenty-third and Twenty-fourth streets. Center for Western Studies photo

Mark Twain Elementary School at Twenty-seventh and Dakota Avenue was next to a cornfield when it was completed in 1921. It was one of several school buildings erected between 1915 and 1923, using this Mediterranean architectural style, when the school board was struggling to keep up with the city's rapid population growth. Center for Western Studies photo

122

The new Whittier Elementary School at 930 East Sixth Street was built in 1924. This building replaced a much smaller school built on the same site in 1882. In 1954 Whittier was converted to a junior high school for grades seven through nine to reduce crowded conditions at nearby Franklin and Bancroft schools and at Washington High School. Center for Western Studies photo

First Lutheran Church, built in 1925 at Twelfth and Dakota, was the last large church to be built in the downtown area. Most older congregations had moved west of Minnesota Avenue and built large new churches prior to 1915. First Lutheran congregation was formed by a union of Grace and St. Olaf congregations in 1920 following a merger of their two church synods in 1917. Thus, not until after 1920 did the new larger congregation undertake the construction of a new church on the site of the former St. Olaf Building. In 1926 the old Grace Lutheran Building was sold to the Mount Zion Jewish congregation. Center for Western Studies photo

The south wing of Washington High School was completed in 1920. Old Central School can be seen still standing between the two wings of the building. In 1935 the final west wing was added and Central School was removed. Center for Western Studies photo

The Ku Klux Klan, shown here at a member's funeral at Woodlawn Cemetery in 1925, was a fairly large and active organization in Sioux Falls in the 1920s. The Argus Leader issue of July 9, 1921 contained an article on the Klan which it reported "is organizing" in Sioux Falls. The Argus ran several editorials explaining that the local Klan was far different from the one in the South. It was, said the Argus, a group dedicated to the maintenance of law and order. In fact, however, most of the local Klan's actions tended to be directed against Catholics. On the night of September 27, 1927, the Tri-state Realm of the Klan meeting, estimated to number between four hundred and five hundred Klansmen, paraded down Phillips Avenue. Later the same night the Klansmen held a rally east of the river on Twenty-sixth Street. The Klan apparently declined in membership and activity after 1928. Center for Western Studies photo

This photo shows the construction of the city's first sewage treatment plant in 1927. Sioux Falls had a population of nearly thirty thousand people in 1925 when it finally approved a six hundred thousand dollar bond issue to construct this sewage plant north of the Morrell Packing Plant. Prior to 1927 the city and Morrell's dumped raw sewage into the Big Sioux River. In dry summers the sewage equalled or exceeded the water flowing from upstream. Center for Western Studies photo

This view shows the electric plant and Morrell's from the Queen Bee Mill in 1928. The hydroelectric plant's generating capacity was supplemented by coal burning, steam driven generators when the electric trolley began operations in Sioux Falls. Eventually steam driven generators were the primary providers of electric power and the water driven generators were used only for back-up. Siouxland Heritage Museums photo

Sherman Park Swimming Area, shown here, in the 1920s, was the first improved swimming facility in Sioux Falls, with the river being damned and lined with retaining walls in 1912-1913. In 1917 the bath house was built. It was the city's only swimming pool until the early Thirties when a swimming area was opened at Covell Lake and the Drake Springs pool was constructed. The trolley line on Twenty-second Street provided transportation to the Sherman Park swimming hole until the trolley ceased operations in 1929. Siouxland Heritage Museums photo

A tree is being planted as the Hills of Rest Cemetery is developed in 1933. This is the most recent of the major cemeteries in Sioux Falls. The first, Mt. Pleasant, was established in 1873. Munce Brothers photo

The new Sioux Valley Hospital at Eighteenth Street and Grange Avenue was completed in 1930. Built by the Sioux Valley Hospital Association, organized in 1925 as a merger of the Sioux Falls and Bethany hospital associations, the new building replaced the hospital at Minnesota and Nineteenth and the Moe Hospital at Fourteenth and Main. The old hospital building on Minnesota Avenue was moved near the new building and used as a nurses' dormitory. William Hoskins photo

The Packard ambulance used at Sioux Valley Hospital in 1930. William Hoskins photo

This view looks east on Ninth Street from the Central Fire Station tower in about 1933. The City Auditorium and Germania Hall would soon be razed to make way for the new Sioux Falls City Hall. The two tallest structures are the Citizens' National Bank and Security National Bank buildings, both built during the prosperous teens. By 1938 only four Sioux Falls banks were in business. Center for Western Studies photo

The old First Baptist Church building was located at Eighth and Dakota in the 1930s. Most of the early churches in the downtown area were converted to business use when their congregations built larger churches in residential areas. Center for Western Studies photo

Drake Springs Swimming Pool is shown here as it appeared in the 1930s. Col. James H. Drake discovered a natural spring on his land east of the river and south of Tenth Street when he drilled a seventy-foot well in 1888. In 1890 Drake offered to supply water to the entire town from this spring, but the city doubted he could furnish enough water for the city's needs and refused the offer. In 1931 the city purchased the property and the next year began constructing a swimming pool. It was completed in 1934. Center for Western Studies photo

The Drake Springs Sunken Gardens was a scenic park area developed near the swimming pool in the 1930s. The garden was removed when the swimming pool was remodeled in the 1960s. Note the old Howard Wood Stadium can be seen in the background. Center for Western Studies photo

The quarry on the Guy Webster farm at Rowena was photographed in the 1930s. Although quartzite had not been used as a building material for over twenty years, several quarries were reopened in the 1930s when WPA projects used quartzite to construct additions to the Federal Post Office Building and Washington High School and to build the Minnehaha Court House Annex. Center for Western Studies photo

The Federal Court House and Post Office Building at Twelfth and Phillips is shown here in 1934. The third floor had been added to the building in 1912-13, and in 1933 a PWA work relief project constructed the annex to the east. These expansions were sufficient to meet Sioux Falls's postal and federal office space needs until the new post office building was completed in 1966. This building now houses only federal court rooms and offices. Center for Western Studies photo

The Morrell Packing Plant and the Sioux Falls Stockyards are shown here in the late twenties or thirties looking east. Although Morrell's was constantly expanding, the area around it was still largely undeveloped except for the Riverside community east of Cliff Avenue and north of Rice Street. Center for Western Studies photo

This photo looks west on Eighth Street from the roof of the Farley-Loetcher Building in 1933. The Farley-Loetcher Company was a millwork manufacturer that began in 1900. From Weber Avenue, in the foreground, to the river are the busy railroad yards and depots. Center for Western Studies photo

The view to the north on Nesmith Avenue was photographed from the roof of the Farley-Loetcher Building in 1933. The Sioux Falls East Side was always a neighborhood of working people who needed to live close to their jobs. This began in 1881 when the Queen Bee built cottages for its employees near the mill and continued with the founding of other industries on or near the East Side like Jordan Millworks in 1884, the Farley-Loetcher Company in 1900, the Manchester Biscuit Company in 1902, and especially the John Morrell Company in 1909. Center for Western Studies photo

The Tenth Street Bridge and Viaduct in 1933, are shown here a year after the new viaduct was constructed. The old viaduct, built in 1890 to allow the East Sioux Falls Trolley to cross the railroad right-of-ways, was unable to accommodate the heavy traffic generated by United States Highway 16. Center for Western Studies photo

This photo of Sixth Street and Main Avenue looks south in 1935. The Queen City Fire Insurance Company at the right, designed by W. L. Dow, was built in 1891-92 by the Baker Brothers. For sometime prior to the mid-1970s the building was the Soo Hotel, but it fell into such disrepair that it was condemned and closed. In the late seventies Architecture Incorporated restored the building to an attractive and functional office facility. It is an excellent example of what can be done to restore the architectural beauty and usefulness of an old building. Center for Western Studies photo

The L and L Motor Supply Company and the Knapp Brown Garage were located on Dakota Avenue between Tenth and Eleventh in 1935-36. L and L, one of the automobile supply pioneers in Sioux Falls, was established in 1917 and is still doing well today. Knapp Brown, an early automobile dealer in Sioux Falls, was also active in promoting aviation in the city. He helped create the first airport in 1929 and managed the Sioux Falls Municipal Airport from 1939 to 1957. Note that Brown's gas pumps are located well into Dakota Avenue. Center for Western Studies photo

The new City Hall was completed in 1936. This building, designed by young architect Harold Spitznagel, is a fine example of the art deco architectural style that was popular in the 1930s. This, like other public buildings constructed in the 1930s, was a WPA project. Center for Western Studies photo

This view looks northwest from the roof of the Citizen's National Bank Building (now occupied by Western Bank) at Ninth and Phillips in about 1937. At that time the J. C. Penney Store was located in the Van Eps Building (with the sign on the wall), but two years later it moved to the former Fantle's Building south of Ninth. The Van Eps Building was torn down in 1969 and practically all the other buildings seen here were razed in the early seventies. Center for Western Studies photo

West Ninth Street was photographed from the roof of the Citizens' National Bank Building (now occupied by Western Bank) at Phillips Avenue in 1938. The new Fantle's Department Store is under construction at the corner of Main Avenue, and across the street is the Security Bank that was robbed of forty-six thousand dollars in 1934 by what may have been the John Dillinger gang. During the robbery "Baby Face" Nelson shot a police officer and the gang made its getaway with hostages forced to ride on the running boards of their Packard to shield them from police bullets. Center for Western Studies photo

Automobile row, seen here in about 1937, was located on Ninth between Minnesota and Dakota avenues. The Bowling Ford Building was the largest garage in South Dakota when it was built in 1919. The Depression had eliminated several of the lesser auto companies. In 1937 you could no longer buy Hupmobile, REO or Essex cars. Center for Western Studies photo

The Sioux Falls College campus is shown here in 1938. Both Sioux Falls College and Augustana College struggled to survive the depressed 1930s. Both benefited greatly from the postwar boom and the returning servicemen eager to gain a college education under the new GI Bill. Few houses were built during the 1930s in Sioux Falls and the photo reveals that the area west of the college was only partially developed in 1938. Sioux Falls College Archives photo

The Japanese Gardens at Terrace Park were first laid out in 1928 and developed under city work relief projects during the Depression. These beautiful gardens were neglected and vandalized after the Japanese attack on Pearl Harbor that began World War II. The swimming pool at the park was built in 1944 by soldiers stationed at the Army Radio School and given to the city when the school closed after the war. Center for Western Studies photo

Howard Wood was a respected coach of football, basketball, and track at Washington High School from 1910 to 1943. Center for Western Studies photo

The Sioux Falls athletic field and track is shown here as it looked in 1939 when it was named Howard Wood Field to honor Washington High School's popular coach of thirty-three years. In 1957 the school district constructed the new Howard Wood Field and sold this one to Sears, Roebuck and Company as a site for its new store that opened in 1961. 1943 Washington High School Yearbook photo

The Sioux Falls Police Department's "cruisers" and paddy wagon in the alley by the new city hall were photographed in about 1939. The department purchased its first automobiles in 1922 and installed the first one-way car radios in 1935. Prior to 1922 the police department used motorcycles or on occasion hired cabs. William Patterson photo

A. N. Graff, mayor of Sioux Falls from 1934-39, led the city through the difficult years of the Depression. He worked hard to secure federal funding for work relief construction projects in Sioux Falls that resulted in the addition of several important public buildings in the city. Of particular importance was his leadership in the establishment of the Sioux Falls Municipal Airport in 1937-39. Photo from Charles A. Smith's Minnehaha County History

The new Sioux Falls Municipal Airport was dedicated on September 15, 1939. The airport, constructed as a WPA project, began the age of commercial air travel in Sioux Falls. In March 1942 the city transferred control of the airport to the federal government along with one thousand adjacent acres of land for the establishment of the Army Radio Technical Training School. Commercial flights continued during the war, and in 1946 the airport facilities were returned to the city. Center for Western Studies photo

The Sioux Falls Motorcycle Police posed for this photo in 1946. The department used motorcycle patrolmen quite extensively from the late teens through the forties. Motorcycles were cheap, fast, and allowed patrolmen to be more accessible to the public than enclosed cars. Sioux Falls Police Department photo

The Modern Boom Period
1941 to 1965

United States entry into World War II in December 1941 began a series of events that dramatically changed Sioux Falls from a provincial agrarian city to a modern urban center. The war stimulated a return to prosperity based on full employment and higher prices for farm goods. But the primary catalyst that ignited a boom period of growth was the establishment of the Army Air Corps Technical Training School in Sioux Falls. The radio school, which trained nearly fifty thousand servicemen during its brief three and one-half year existence, stimulated the city's population growth in the 1940s, and that momentum continued through the decade of the fifties before leveling off in the 1960s. In the twenty years after 1940 the city's population grew faster than ever before, adding roughly twelve thousand people to the census totals in each of the two decades. As a result, the city experienced a frenzy of building unlike anything it had known since the frontier boom times of the 1880s. It seemed as if cornfields gave way to new residential developments overnight and that dusty country roads became paved city streets the following day. In the postwar period new wholesale distributors and manufacturing businesses took up residence in the industrial park made from the abandoned radio school. Church congregations that had moved from the downtown and built larger church buildings in the teens moved again in the fifties to new residential neighborhoods and built even larger buildings. The school district, facing perhaps the greatest challenge of the postwar population boom, constructed new elementary schools, established a new system of junior high schools to temporarily relieve pressure on Washington High School, and in the end built a second high school

This air photo of Sioux Falls in 1943 shows the Army Radio School at the top stretching from Covell Lake to the airport. The school's impact on Sioux Falls was tremendous. Five thousand men were hired to construct the facility in a three month period. They installed thirty miles of sewer and water lines, seventeen miles of streets, and erected over eight hundred buildings including barracks, classroom buildings, eighteen warehouses, three chapels, and an eight-hundred-bed hospital facility. Siouxland Heritage Museums photo

in the rapidly growing suburban area south of the downtown. Downtown Sioux Falls enjoyed unparalleled business as the region's paramount retail shopping center during the fifties, but the city's sprawling growth made almost inevitable the rise of the suburban shopping center by the late sixties.

In the same way that the coming of railroads launched the boom time of the 1880s, the coming of the Army Radio School launched the modern boom of the forties and fifties. The Roosevelt administration's war preparedness program made rapid mobilization possible after December 7, 1941. The army, knowing it would need thousands of radio technicians and operators, was ready to establish training schools as soon as Congress declared war. When the city learned the federal government was seeking a site for a radio training school, it moved quickly to offer the Municipal Airport and an additional thousand acres of land it purchased. By March 1942, the government had accepted the city's offer and construction of the training facility began. During the next three months, five thousand workers were hired to construct the equivalent of a small city virtually from scratch. Streets, sewer, water and electrical systems were installed, and, of course, barracks, classroom buildings, administrative and other support buildings were erected in which to house and train sixteen thousand men at a time. Airport runways were strengthened and lengthened to handle the larger military aircraft.

The employment situation in the Sioux Falls area changed overnight. Unemployment virtually disappeared and people flocked to Sioux Falls to get the well-paying construction jobs. When the construction phase was complete, the military draft provided continued employment for many of the workers for the duration.

In July 1942 the soldiers began arriving, and the radio school began converting them into radio operator technicians. At its high point the school "enrolled" twenty-seven thousand men with classes running on three rotating shifts during each twenty-four hour day. This sudden increase in population both stimulated and strained the Sioux Falls economy and social institutions. The base itself required hundreds of civilian employees to work in its numerous canteens, barbershops, gas stations, theatres and other support facilities. But the main economic impact was felt in downtown Sioux Falls. The soldiers could leave the base during off hours, and on their one day off per week they crowded stores, bars, restaurants and dance halls. This extraordinary wartime business allowed enterprising businessmen to expand and to gather the assets that became the foundation of their postwar success.

Housing was already scarce in Sioux Falls when the war began, and the war effort permitted only minimal civilian construction. Consequently, the influx of people after the spring of 1942 put a terrible strain upon the housing situation. In addition to the hundreds of people who came to seek jobs directly or indirectly related to the radio school's presence, hundreds of wives and children came to Sioux Falls to be near their husbands and fathers during their eighteen to twenty-six week training period. In time virtually every house in town rented rooms, and in some cases rooms were divided by temporary partitions to create additional accommodations for the swollen wartime population.

On the last day of 1945, more than four months after the end of the war, the radio school was closed, and soon after the land and its facilities were returned

to the city of Sioux Falls. Many of the 950 radio school buildings were dismantled, but more than 450 were sold for 5 percent of their appraised value. Building materials that had been almost non-existent during the war years continued to be scarce in the postwar period. Consequently, the availability of the radio school buildings was a boon to the city. Area colleges acquired buildings for classrooms and dormitories to accommodate the dramatic increase in student enrollment caused by returning GIs with veteran's educational benefits. Several church congregations in new suburban neighborhoods solved their need for a church building by purchasing and moving radio school chapels to new sites. Barracks became private homes in several new areas of the city, and lumber from radio school buildings made the construction of other new houses possible.

The radio school also provided the city with much improved municipal airport facilities and the basis for a new industrial park. Acquisition of the vast acreage north of Madison Street and Covell Lake, made possible by the wartime emergency, allowed the city to re-enter the competition for new industry in the expansive prosperity of the postwar period with real advantages over many rival cities. It possessed several hundred acres of land that already contained basic city services. The city could offer prospective industries this land at attractive prices, and in many cases the land included ready-made structures in which to begin business. The Industrial and Development Foundation of the Chamber of Commerce began a vigorous campaign to bring new industries to this area, and its efforts were successful in filling the industrial park with new businesses during the fifties and sixties.

The federal government continued to provide the city important support in the postwar period. The government purchased the former Columbus College Building and dedicated it as a veteran's hospital in 1949, adding a large new medical facility to the city. And in 1955 local businessmen and government officials travelled to Washington, D.C., to convince Congress to fund a large scale flood control project to tame the Big Sioux River as it flowed through the city. Unfortunately, the project, which had been sought for more than a decade, was begun too late to save the city from the flood of 1957, the worst since the great flood of 1881. The Army Corps of Engineers' project not only straightened and widened the river channel and built high dikes along its banks, it also removed the old Cascade Mill Dam at Eighth Street thereby lowering the water level through the downtown area. The key feature of the flood control system was a dam north of the city that regulated the volume of water flowing through the city by diverting excess amounts down the diversion channel and spillway to the river below the downtown area.

Construction of downtown Sioux Falls was essentially completed by 1920. Aside from the Fantle's store in 1938 and the Woolworth store in 1941, few new buildings were constructed in the downtown during the 1930s and 1940s. By 1950, despite its being a booming retail center, the downtown was in need of refurbishing. Old-fashioned facades were "modernized" with plastic, glass tile or metal coverings, but behind the new fronts old buildings remained. Some areas of the downtown that contained old frame structures were in rundown and dilapidated condition. Moreover, the growing number of shoppers driving cars downtown encountered serious parking problems. Instead of renovating or replacing old buildings many established businesses began moving from the downtown to new quarters along South Minnesota

This is another view of the Army Radio School in 1943. The dark objects in the center are rows of the tar paper covered barracks, and running down the middle are the larger, darker colored classroom buildings. On the extreme left is the hospital area. Black soldiers were separately housed in a small barracks complex at the upper left of the main barracks area. Many of these structures were sold to private individuals and organizations after the war and moved to new locations. Several of the buildings are in use in the industrial park, at the two colleges in Sioux Falls and at other places in the community. Siouxland Heritage Museums photo

Captain Joe Foss posed with his wife and mother upon his return home to Sioux Falls in 1945. Foss became a national hero during the war as a Marine fighter pilot who equalled Eddie Rickenbacker's World War I record of shooting down twenty-six enemy planes. Shot down and rescued three times, Foss was awarded the Congressional Medal of Honor. After the war he commanded the South Dakota Air National Guard in Sioux Falls, and in 1955 the Sioux Falls Municipal Airport was named Joe Foss Field in his honor. In 1954 Foss was elected Governor of South Dakota for the first of two terms, and in 1960 he became commissioner of the American Football League. Foss is now retired and lives in Arizona. Center for Western Studies photo

This 1940 view of the west side of Phillips Avenue between Tenth and Ninth streets shows the Newberry Store that had been built in 1916-17 and next to it the Woolworth Store that was still in the old C. K. Howard Building. In 1941 Woolworth's moved into a new building that replaced three old stores in the middle of the block. Center for Western Studies photo

Avenue or to other suburban areas where ample customer parking could be provided.

Although the real rush of downtown businesses to the suburbs did not occur until the sixties, the beginnings of this trend occurred in the late 1940s and 1950s. Hutton-Tufty Chrysler and Dodge, the first auto dealership to leave the downtown for roomier accommodations, relocated on South Minnesota Avenue in 1947. Three years later the Sunshine Mutual Insurance Company constructed its new headquarters at 22nd Street and Minnesota Avenue. In 1949, the city's first suburban shopping mall, Southway, began the movement that ultimately destroyed the downtown's monopoly on retail shopping. The shopping mall is simply a modern, larger version of the corner grocery designed to save the suburbanite the inconvenience of travelling downtown to shop. Lewis Drug, which had opened its first store downtown in 1942, opened the largest drug store in South Dakota at 35th Street and Minnesota Avenue in 1956. Jordan Millworks, which had been downtown since the 1880s, moved to the new industrial park near the airport in 1957. Six years later, the Kresge Company opened its new K-Mart store at 37th Street and Minnesota Avenue.

The rapid population increase of the forties stimulated a church building boom in the fifties. East Side Lutheran and Christ the King erected new buildings in 1950. First Baptist left its old building downtown for a larger structure at 22nd Street and Covell Avenue in 1951, and First Presbyterian sold its old downtown building to the Seventh Day Adventists and constructed a new church on South West Avenue in 1955. Several new congregations, organized in the suburbs, constructed new churches in the late fifties and early sixties.

The population pressure of the postwar period quickly came to bear upon the public school system. Washington High School, the only public high school in the city, literally bulged at the seams by the early fifties. More than twenty-five hundred students attended classes in the block-large quartzite building. To alleviate this pressure on Washington High the district decided to create a system of junior high schools. Whittier Elementary School was remodeled and two new buildings, Edison and Axtell Park, were opened as junior high schools in 1954, taking seventh and eighth graders from the elementary schools and ninth graders from Washington High. Three years later a fourth

junior high, Patrick Henry, was opened. Despite the four new junior high schools, the twelve thousand new residents added to the city in the 1950s forced the city to construct a new high school in 1965. In the year before Lincoln High School opened, Washington High School operated on two shifts to accommodate more than three thousand high school students.

Sioux Falls, like most of the nation, entered the television age in the 1950s. In May 1953 the Midcontinent Broadcasting Company began the KELO television station, and seven years later Morton Henkin, owner of KSOO radio, launched a second television station in the city. Several radio people, notably Dave Dedrick (Captain Eleven), made the transition to television and experienced first hand the swift technological improvements of the media. Television required a far greater investment in personnel and equipment than radio, and that in turn required a large market area to make the investment profitable. Sioux Falls was the only city in the area in which commercial television was feasible in the 1950s. Consequently, television, like radio, became a Sioux Falls industry and increased its stature as a regional urban center.

The population growth of the forties and fifties enabled the city to support new cultural organizations and construct new public athletic facilities in the early sixties. In 1960, the local Town and Gown Symphony Orchestra, an outgrowth of the Augustana College Orchestra, became the Sioux Falls Symphony with a community board of directors and growing community support. The Sioux Falls Chamber of Commerce became a supporter of the Sioux Falls Symphony after IBM decided to locate its new plant in Rochester, Minnesota, rather than in Sioux Falls, in part because of Rochester's superior cultural atmosphere. The next year, 1961, the Civic Fine Arts Center organized and opened the first public art gallery in Sioux Falls. Utilizing some of the former radio school land, the city developed a complex of municipal athletic facilities beginning with the new Howard Wood Field in 1957, the Arena in 1962, and the Packer Baseball Stadium in 1965.

World War II enabled the American people to make money when there was little they could buy. After the war this pent-up buying power produced a genuine spending spree, and one of the things many people wanted most was a new car. By the fifties Detroit was turning out cars in record numbers every year and they were getting bigger, more powerful and

141

This 1945 photo of Eighth and Phillips Avenue looks south. Few changes occurred to the streets of Sioux Falls during the war because the war effort did not permit new civilian construction. Government controls kept prices reasonable. A room at the Cataract Hotel was one dollar and fifty cents per night and a movie ticket was only twenty-five cents. Richard Munce photo

faster. Moreover gasoline was cheap. Just as autos had spawned repair garages and filling stations in the twenties and thirties, in the forties and fifties they gave rise to the drive-in restaurant and the drive-in movie theater. The Barrell Drive-In Restaurant on South Minnesota Avenue opened in 1939 and the East Park and Starlight drive-in theaters were erected in 1948. The drive-in restaurant's popularity peaked in the late fifties and early sixties before the modern fast food franchise chains took over.

Local, state, and federal governments worked desperately to improve streets and roads to keep pace with the growing number of cars. By the mid-fifties Congress began plans for constructing a network of superhighways across the nation. Sen. Karl E. Mundt of South Dakota was one of those involved in drawing out on a map the proposed routes of these new interstate highways. This time, unlike the nineteenth century when transcontinental railroads missed South Dakota, two major interstate highways crossed the state and they intersected at Sioux Falls. Between 1961 and 1963 Interstates 29 and 90 as well as the

beltway 229 were completed around the city. (The final stretch of interstate construction in the state was not completed until the early 1980s.) Being the intersection of two interstate highways meant Sioux Falls was and would remain a regional transportation center. It meant that the city could attract industries that depended upon easy highway accessibility, and that regional shoppers and tourists would continue to build the city's retail trade. Moreover the interstates made Sioux Falls less dependent upon the deteriorating railroad service. In 1965 the last passenger train left Sioux Falls signaling the final victory of the automobile and the federally-funded highway over the railroad in the business of transporting people.

The year 1965 is a dividing point in the modern history of Sioux Falls. The downtown still enjoyed a virtual monopoly on retail trade in the city, and its nineteenth and early twentieth century buildings remained essentially intact. Federally-funded urban renewal, the interstate highways and the continuous sprawl of the city would change all that in the years that followed.

Starting on the right at Ninth and moving south on Phillips Avenue in 1945 are the Minnehaha Building, Montgomery Ward's and J. C. Penney's. In 1935 Montgomery Ward's moved into the building that had been occupied by the Freese-Rohde Department Store, and J. C. Penney's relocated to the Fantle Building in 1939 when Fantle's moved to its new building at Main and Ninth. Richard Munce photo

The Cataract Hotel is shown here as it appeared in 1945. The entire downtown was starting to look old and a little run down by the end of the war. Few new buildings had been built downtown since 1921 and postwar building shortages postponed new construction for the next two to three years. Richard Munce photo

This view shows Tenth and Phillips looking south in 1945. The major change on this segment of Phillips was the razing of the old Masonic Temple in 1929 to make way for the new S. S. Kresge Five and Ten Cent Store. Richard Munce photo

Morton Henkin (1911-1974), son of the pioneer of commercial radio in Sioux Falls, Joseph Henkin, founded the second television station in Sioux Falls, KSOO-TV. KSOO, later KSFY-TV, began broadcasting on July 31, 1960. Photo courtesy of Sylvia Henkin

This photo of Eleventh and Phillips Avenue looks south in 1945. The Palace of Sweets on the corner was a popular spot for Washington High students after school and also for soldiers from the Radio School on their day off. Lewis Drug had opened its first store downtown in 1942. Just past the Lewis Drug Store and the Northern States Power Building is the KSOO radio station. In 1926 Joe Henkin started KSOO when radio was still new and paying

advertisers hard to find. To make money the station ran a program that gave advise on personal problems sent in along with a dollar by listeners. In 1937, the year KSOO moved to this location on south Phillips, Henkin started KELO radio to operate in the evening while KSOO continued to broadcast only during the daytime. In 1947 the Federal Communications Commission ordered Henkin to sell one of the stations. Richard Munce photo

The notable addition to this block was the State Theater which opened in 1926. With a stage and a seating capacity of 1,350 it was—and still is—the largest theater in South Dakota. This view taken in 1945 looks north on Phillips Avenue from Twelfth Street. Richard Munce photo

The north side of Twelfth Street between Main and Phillips in 1945 was photographed shortly before these buildings were razed. Several of these frame structures had been moved to this location from Phillips Avenue when they had been replaced by larger structures in the 1880s. R. F. Pettigrew's original land office, for instance, is the fourth building from the left. It had been erected in the spring of 1871 between Seventh and Eighth streets on Phillips Avenue. Center for Western Studies photo

The Emerson Block, built in 1891, is on the corner while further down the street is the Chocolate Shop, a popular spot for the younger crowd, especially during Prohibition. The First National Bank Building, erected in 1929, stands in the middle of the block in this 1945 photo looking south at Ninth and Phillips. Richard Munce photo

The new Woolworth Store, built in 1941 between Ninth and Tenth on Phillips Avenue, was the first store building in Sioux Falls equipped with air conditioning. It is seen here in 1945. Richard Munce photo

Kopel's Store on the corner of Tenth and Phillips had just received its facelift in 1947. Next door is the original Sunshine Food Market started in 1931 by George Sercl. Sunshine Markets would soon be built outside the downtown area to be closer to customers and provide them easier parking. Parking meters had just been installed on downtown streets. Richard Munce photo

The Augustana College Campus is shown here as it appeared about 1949. Augustana College, like most colleges, was experiencing a postwar boom in enrollment as young people returned to civilian life after the war. The college solved its space problems by acquiring several barracks and a large classroom building from the deactivated Army Radio School. The barracks, which served as dormitories and the school cafeteria, are at the upper middle of the photo and the classroom building is in the lower left corner. Augustana College Archive photo

This is the Royal C. Johnson Veterans Memorial Hospital as it appeared in the early 1950s. During World War II the Veterans Administration purchased the grounds and buildings of the former Columbus College and in 1946 began construction of the main hospital building in the foreground. It was completed in 1949 and the facility named after Royal C. Johnson, a South Dakota native who was instrumental in creating the Veterans Administration. Siouxland Heritage Museums photo

146

First Baptist Church, completed in 1951 on West Twenty-second Street, is typical of several downtown churches that built new and larger church buildings in the rapidly expanding residential areas in the fifties. Indeed, the 1950s saw a virtual wave of church building as the city's population explosion in the post war period was reflected in new or enlarged congregations all needing new houses of worship. Center for Western Studies photo

A fire swept through the Queen Bee Mill in 1956, and in 1961—for safety reasons—the walls were knocked down to the first floor. The mill, built in 1879-81, as the most modern flour mill in the entire Midwest, ran only about a dozen years during its existence. Siouxland Heritage Museums photo

The top four floors of the Edmison-Jamison Block had been removed in 1947 for fire safety reasons. The remainder of this once majestic building also received the typical postwar "modernization" of its first floor facade. The Argus Leader *noted on July 22, 1947, that "This is the first major construction project in the downtown in several years." This is how it looked in 1951. Richard Munce photo*

Dave Dedrick made a successful transition from radio to television when the first television station, KELO (Channel 11) began in 1953. A well-liked weather man, Dedrick is perhaps best known as Captain Eleven, host since 1955 of an afternoon children's cartoon show. KELO Television Station photo

The Barrell Drive-In Restaurant, at Thirty-first Street and Minnesota Avenue, looked like this in 1955. Started in 1939 by Lloyd Eagan in a barrel-shaped building, the Barrell proved popular with the younger generation that was increasingly mobile in their own or the family car. The Barrell was the first restaurant in Sioux Falls to serve french fries, and success after

the war prompted Eagan to build a larger building. Most drive-in restaurants and theaters in Sioux Falls, including the Barrell, closed in the 1970s as victims of national fast food chains and air conditioning. The last drive-in theater, the Starlight, closed in 1985. Lloyd Eagan photo

Lloyd Eagan (right), Richard Beck and car hops on a busy afternoon at the Barrell Drive-In in the fifties. Lloyd Eagan photo

149

The new Patrick Henry Junior High School was completed in 1957. This was the last of the four junior highs opened by the school district in the 1950s as it adopted a separate junior high system to relieve pressure on both elementary schools and Washington High School. Patrick Henry was to serve the rapidly growing southeast section of the city. Joel Strasser photo

The Hilltop Area, a new residential development section, grew rapidly in the 1950s because of low interest loans available to veterans under the GI Bill. East Park Drive-In Theatre, which opened in 1948, can be seen in the grove of trees in the background. The Cleveland School is also visible in this 1958 photo. Joel Strasser photo

O'Gorman High School was completed in 1962. The construction of this school at Kiwanis and Forty-first Street greatly accelerated residential development of the adjacent area east of Kiwanis Avenue. The school, recently cited by the United States Department of Education as one of the best high schools in the country, enrolled nearly seven hundred students in the fall of 1985. N.S.P. Horizons, Sioux Falls in the 70's photo

The Dickenson Bakery and Confectionary on Main Avenue between Tenth and Eleventh was photographed shortly before it was torn down about 1958. R. W. "Dad" Dickenson, founder of the bakery, learned his trade in England and came to Sioux Falls in 1888. Dickenson, an unusual man in his personal appearance with hair down to his shoulders, a long white coat reaching below his knees and high boots, was also unusual for the buildings he constructed. His house near Tenth Street and Cliff Avenue was inspired by a dream and had no square corners, and this building was often referred to as the "Katzenjammer Castle" after the popular comic strip. Despite his eccentricities, Dickenson was beloved by the community as a generous and warm-hearted man. Dickenson died in 1916 and his sons continued the business until the early 1950s. Center for Western Studies photo

This photo looks west on Ninth from Phillips Avenue in 1960. The Hollister-Beveridge Building, just west of the Cataract had been removed in 1956 to make room for Fantle's Parking Ramp, and some of the buildings had received first floor facelifts, but few major changes had occurred in the downtown during the previous two decades. Sioux Falls Traffic Department photo

Senator John F. Kennedy campaigned for the presidency at the National Plowing Contest near Sioux Falls in September of 1960. His appearance failed to prevent Richard Nixon from carrying South Dakota in the November election. Joel Strasser photo

Wayne Pritchard's voice has been part of getting up and ready for work and school in Sioux Falls since 1948. He arrived in town to work for radio station KIHO only to find it impossible to secure a place for his family to live. To dramatize the city's postwar housing shortgage, Pritchard lived in, and broadcast from the display window of the Shriver-Johnson Department Store for nearly a week. Pritchard began his career at KSOO in 1955. Photo courtesy of KSOO Radio

Southway, the earliest retail "mall" development outside the downtown, had its beginning in 1938 when Strong Florists built a greenhouse on south Minnesota Avenue. The next year Arthur and Eunice Anderson purchased the property and ran the greenhouse to support their flower shop on south Main Avenue. In 1948 the Andersons began the development of Southway shopping mall when they constructed a building in which Sam Hagger and sons opened a grocery store. The photo shows the new Anderson Flower Shop shortly after it opened in 1952-53. Photo courtesy Arthur Anderson family

The Cataract Hotel's exterior had been "modernized" by 1960 and the downtown was enjoying its last years as the main retail center of the region before the advent of the large suburban shopping malls. This photo shows Phillips Avenue looking north from Ninth Street. Sioux Falls Traffic Department photo

The downtown was still thriving, but the exodus of businesses to Minnesota Avenue and other suburban locations was beginning about 1960 when Phillips Avenue was photographed looking north from the roof of the Shriver Building on Eleventh. Center for Western Studies photo

This is the intersection of Tenth and Minnesota in the winter of 1960-61. Until the completion of the interstate highways around the city in 1963 this was the intersection of Highways 16 and 77, the two busiest highways in the state. Sioux Falls Traffic Department photo

This view of Minnesota Avenue looks north from Thirty-fourth Street in about 1962. In the 1960s Minnesota Avenue began to replace Phillips Avenue as the main retail street in Sioux Falls. Shown here being widened to four lanes, the street, once residential, was rapidly commercialized in the late fifties and sixties. A similar process occurred on west Forty-first Street in the seventies. Sioux Falls Traffic Department photo

The Sioux Falls Sports Complex was photographed in 1962. The Arena had just been completed, Howard Wood Field had been moved from east Tenth (the site of the Sears, Roebuck Store) in 1957, and the Packer Baseball Stadium would be constructed in 1965. This area, part of the Army Radio School grounds, had reverted to the city after the war. Note the lack of development along West Avenue and Russell Street. Center for Western Studies photo

The Interstate 29 and Interstate 90 interchange northwest of Sioux Falls was completed in 1962. Sioux Falls was fortunate to be on the route of two of the super highways authorized by Congress in the 1950s. It guaranteed that the city would continue to be a transportation center in the auto and truck age by providing excellent connections to the region and beyond. Joel Strasser photo

West Twelfth Street would soon be widened to four lanes to cope with the increasing traffic caused by its commercial development. This is how it appeared in 1962 looking east. Sioux Falls Traffic Department photo

The Sioux Falls Stockyards are shown here in 1963. Prior to 1917, when the stockyards were founded, area farmers had to ship their livestock by rail to St. Paul, Chicago, or Sioux City. The presence of John Morrell Company in Sioux Falls after 1909 helped make a local stockyard feasible. Drawing on a large livestock producing region, the Sioux Falls Stockyards grew steadily until it became the nation's largest in 1982. Today the stockyards consist of forty-six acres of pens and supporting facilities including a bank, cafe, western clothing store and two of the Midwest's largest commodity offices. Joel Strasser photo

This photo of Tenth and Phillips looks north in 1965. The old C. K. Howard Store on the far left and all the other buildings on that side of the street to Ninth would be gone by the end of the next decade as the downtown adjusted to the rising popularity of the suburban shopping malls. Center for Western Studies photo

Lincoln High School was completed in 1965. Marking yet another move of the community away from the downtown area, Lincoln reduced the student enrollment pressure on Washington High School. Between 1948 and 1965 Sioux Falls constructed ten new schools to keep up with the city's growing population. Photo from the Lincoln Senior High School 1967 Heritage

The Milwaukee Road's Arrow Passenger Train left Sioux Falls for the last time in 1965. Sioux Falls, never on a transcontinental railroad route, was unable to support railroad passenger service in the age of interstate highway and air travel. The departure of the Arrow was the end of an era. Joel Strasser photo

The Great Plains Zoo on Kiwanis Avenue opened in 1963. This was the first zoo in Sioux Falls to feature animals not native to South Dakota. R. F. Pettigrew had created a zoo that included buffalo, elk and prairie dogs at South Sioux Falls in 1890, but the last buffalo was sold to Buffalo, New York, when the "Buffalo Park" was closed in 1894. In this century the city began in the 1920s to maintain a collection of native animals in a fenced area at both Terrace and Sherman parks. This photo shows the zoo after the addition of the Children's Park in 1970. Joel Strasser photo

The Western Mall was photographed shortly after its completion in the fall of 1968. With plenty of free parking, a climate controlled environment and a large variety of stores, several of which had formerly been downtown including Montgomery Ward's, the opening the of Western Mall marked the beginning of the end for the downtown as the city's major retail shopping center. Note the lack of development along Western Avenue and Forty-first Street at the time. That would come rapidly as the shopping traffic focused more and more on this corner of the city. *Western Mall photo*

The Remaking of Sioux Falls
1965 to 1987

Sioux Falls experienced fundamental and profound changes in the two decades after 1965. These changes were more dramatic than any the city had ever experienced since the coming of the first railroad in 1878. The result has been the essential remaking of the city. The three major elements of this change have been urban renewal, shopping malls and high technology. The first element, the remaking of the downtown, was stimulated and made possible by an infusion of federal urban-renewal money. The development of large retail shopping malls was simply the culmination of trends begun earlier. But it is high technology that in the long run may have the most profound impact on Sioux Falls. Computers and satellite communications have come to have equal importance to easy highway or air access in the success of the largest new industries to locate in Sioux Falls. With the aid of new state usury and banking laws, Sioux Falls has attracted these new computer-age industries in much the same way it attracted those that relied upon railroads and highways in the past.

The remaking of downtown Sioux Falls began in 1965 when the First Bank of South Dakota razed the old Syndicate/Western Surety Block at the corner of Eighth and Main and replaced it with a modern ten-story bank and office building. The next year the federal government began its role in changing the face of the downtown area by clearing an entire block of old run-down structures to make way for the new Post Office Building between Eleventh and Twelfth streets on Second Avenue. But the real impact of the federal

This photo of Downtown Sioux Falls in 1965 looks toward the northwest. The beginning of major rebuilding of the downtown began in 1965 with the removal of two larrge nineteenth-century buildings: the Syndicate/Western Surety Building at Eighth and Main and the Metropolitan Block at the corner of Tenth and Main. Center for Western Studies photo

The Pathfinder Nuclear Generating Plant east of Sioux Falls is shown here in 1966. Built that year by Northern States Power Company in cooperation with other power companies, as an experimental facility, the plant ran for little more than a year. It did, however, provide important experience and information for the design of future nuclear-powered electric plants. Joel Strasser photo

an urban renewal program designed to rebuild the decaying cities of America. Sioux Falls had to meet certain organizational and planning prerequisites before the federal money began to flow, and thus it took some time before the local urban-renewal program got underway. The need for renewal of the downtown became increasingly apparent as business began moving to the new shopping mall that opened in 1968.

In the fall of 1968 the city's first major shopping mall, the Western Mall, opened at Forty-first Street and Western Avenue, an area commercially undeveloped at the time. As the focus of shopping traffic began to shift away from downtown to the Western Mall, more and more businesses opened on Forty-first Street to benefit from this traffic. Forty-first Street quickly began to evolve from a residential street to the new business-strip of the city with the opening of small specialty shops in converted houses and the building of numerous fast-food restaurants. Traffic and congestion increased in proportion and compelled the city to make major street improvements in the mall area.

The Western Mall gradually caused the retail shopping trade to move from downtown to the southwestern edge of the city. The mall attracted new businesses to the city, but it also attracted established downtown stores as well. Montgomery Wards, which had been in the old Bee Hive Store Building on Phillips Avenue since 1935, became one of the original "anchor stores" of the Western Mall while Tempo, a new discount department store, anchored the mall's other end. The same mixture of new and old was true of smaller stores in the mall as well. By 1973 the Western Mall's success prompted it to build a major addition to the south and the new space was quickly filled with retail stores.

With the shopping traffic moving away from the downtown and toward the Western Mall, downtown merchants and city officials struggled to "save the downtown." With the aid of massive amounts of federal urban-renewal funds, the city launched a removal and rebuilding program that literally remade the downtown. The scope and speed of the transformation, while impressive at the time, is almost breathtaking when summarized in retrospect.

City planners first attacked the problem of too-little parking in the downtown area. Beginning in 1971 an entire two block, old wholesale warehouse section was razed east of Phillips Avenue between Ninth and Eleventh streets, and the area was paved into municipal parking lots. The sole survivor of this massive removal program was the old Rock Island Depot which was renovated into a restaurant.

In 1971 the renewal of the area north of Eighth Street and west of the river to Dakota Avenue was begun. In that year the city cleared a block of dilapidated frame structures between Main and Dakota avenues to make way for a new Public Library and parking. In 1972 the Downtown Holiday Inn replaced a block of old frame buildings between Main and Phillips avenues, the River Tower Apartments were constructed, and the west half of the block north of the new library was cleared to erect the first half of a projected twin office building called the Court House Plaza.

In 1973 the urban renewal program turned its focus south of Eighth Street and the results were equally dramatic. The Cataract Hotel, Lincoln Hotel (northeast corner of Ninth and Main), the two buildings between them and the other structures along Main and Phillips on the same block were razed. The old Van Eps Block on the northeast corner of the

Cataract Hotel block had been taken down in 1969. Consequently, by 1974 the entire city block between Eighth and Ninth and Main and Phillips had been cleared. In the Cataract's historic site at the corner of Ninth and Phillips a new large bank and office building was constructed in 1974 with most of the rest of the block given over to parking. Large portions of other blocks south of Eighth Street were also cleared for parking.

Another strategy, begun in 1973 to lure shoppers back to the downtown, was the creation of a pedestrian mall on Phillips Avenue between Ninth and Eleventh streets. Architects first proposed an enclosed mall to protect shoppers from the elements, but the city opted for a less expensive open air mall instead. The street was removed and new pavement, trees, sandboxes, exhibit boxes and benches were installed for pedestrian traffic only. The downtown now had parking and a pedestrian mall, but it continued to lose both stores and shoppers.

In 1975 Sioux Falls acquired a second major shopping mall when developers decided to construct an even larger retail mall west, across the river from the Western Mall. While the new Empire Mall brought Younker's and eventually Dayton's to the city for the first time, it also enticed J. C. Penney into leaving the downtown to become one of its "anchor stores." Fantle's, too, moved to the Empire leaving Shriver's as the sole downtown department store.

The addition of the Empire Mall accelerated the development of Forty-first Street. During the 1970s every auto dealership except one left the downtown for larger, roomier quarters, and all but the Chevrolet and AMC dealers relocated on west Forty-first Street. The increased traffic generated by the second mall required the city to widen Forty-first Street to six lanes.

Restaurants, grocery stores, motels, more fast-food restaurants and apartment buildings gradually appeared along west Forty-first Street.

Retail development in the southwest area of the city continued with the addition of a third shopping mall, the New Town Mall, in 1980. This shopping complex, just east of the Empire Mall used the Target Store, built in 1979, as its "anchor" and attracted Shriver's as its other major department store. Shriver's, the last department store to leave the downtown, had moved into the Western Mall in 1979, and thus the New Town Mall was a second location. After quickly filling most of its retail space, the New Town Mall began a steady decline, a trend that was also affecting the older Western Mall. The high interest rates of the early eighties and the declining farm economy were undoubtedly major causes of the closing of shop after shop in the Western and New Town malls leaving large portions of each empty. It may also be true that the retail sector in Sioux Falls had become overbuilt for the existing consumer market.

As major shopping malls continued to grow on the southwest edge of the city and smaller ones were added in other neighborhoods, the downtown continued to change. In 1976 a third bank building was constructed at the intersection of Ninth and Phillips when the First National Bank replaced its old structure, saving only the giant stone eagle. In 1979 the Midland Life Insurance Company moved to Sioux Falls and constructed a large glass office building one block east of Phillips Avenue near the river. The fourth corner of Ninth and Phillips received a bank building in 1980 when the Block Eleven Redevelopment Project began and the remaining old buildings on the west side of Phillips, south of Ninth Street, were removed. The Block Eleven Project later added a parking ramp, but efforts to attract a developer willing to construct a major new hotel on the remainder of the block were repeatedly unsuccessful. In 1985 the city voted down a plan to construct a new hotel and convention center on the east side of Phillips Avenue south of the First National Bank Building. This plan would have removed the remaining old structures in the block on that side of Phillips Avenue. But even without this proposed convention center project, the events of the two decades after 1965 have clearly remade the downtown from an established and successful retail center to a banking and office district.

By the late 1960s a national reaction had occurred to the wholesale destruction through federal urban-renewal programs of old buildings having architectural and historic importance. As a result, Congress established the National Register of Historic Buildings and Places, amended the federal tax code to provide incentives for the restoration and penalties for the demolition of historic structures, and provided funds to assist communities and individuals in restoring buildings placed on the National Register.

Sioux Falls launched its historic preservation movement in 1975 with the local museum board designated as the local historic preservation board. The tax incentives and limited amounts of federal renovation funds had their impact. The Van Brunt Building, Albert Hotel, Soo Square, Illinois Central Depot, and Kuehn Warehouse are examples of private owners using these incentives to restore old buildings and adapt them to new uses. Residential areas, too, specifically the Cathedral and McKennan Park neighborhoods, were declared historic districts and many of their houses have been restored to their former grandeur. Perhaps the most important and prominent example of historic preservation in Sioux Falls is the Old County Court House at Sixth and Main. Spared the wrecker's ball when it was abandoned for the new court house in 1962, despite the *Argus Leader* editorializing (September 11, 1962) to replace it with a parking lot, the Old Court House has been retained as a local architectural treasure and is being restored to serve the community as a museum and a meeting place. The buildings that surround the Old Court House from Main Avenue to the river, and from the south side of Sixth Street to Fifth Street have also been placed on the National Register to protect the historic setting of the Old Court House. The architectural heritage of this area of the city will be preserved for generations as the buildings are restored and continue to serve useful functions.

A lack of revenue had made it difficult for Sioux Falls to sponsor municipal cultural institutions. Thus a significant event of the period after 1965 was the adoption of a city sales tax in 1969. The initial one-half percent tax was increased to one percent the next year, and this new income allowed the city to support some new projects. One of these was the creation in 1974 of the joint city-county museum system, bringing together the city's Pettigrew Museum and the county's newly created Old Court House Museum under one director and staff. The new system, named the Siouxland Heritage Museums, undertook an extensive program of creating new, professional quality exhibits and implemented a long-range plan for the restoration of the two museum buildings. From these efforts Sioux Falls has acquired a quality museum system dedicated to preserving the community's history and relating it to visitors of all ages through interpretive exhibits and publications.

Sioux Falls opened its new air terminal building in 1970 as it sought to maintain its position as the air travel center for this four-state region. The airport facilities that the city acquired from the federal government at the end of World War II were inadequate by the 1960s, and federal money again helped with construction costs. The new Costello Terminal increased the number of airlines serving Sioux Falls and air connections to nearly all parts of the country improved. The advantages of possessing a modern air terminal facility have been important to the city's continued growth. Modern businesses require fast airmail and freight service, and the ability to travel easily and quickly to distant cities for sales meetings and conferences. Indeed, a spokesman for a Texas banking corporation, that recently relocated its credit card operation in Sioux Falls, stated that one of the reasons his company chose Sioux Falls is its excellent air service. Being on national airline routes, like being on interstate highways, means Sioux Falls is easily accessible. It also makes it the entry and departure point for the surrounding region. (*Argus Leader*, October 28, 1984).

The key to any city's success is its ability to keep current with new trends. This can be seen in Sioux Falls's experience with railroads, highways and airports. It is equally true for the most recent trend in

The USS Battleship South Dakota Memorial is located in Sherman Park at Kiwanis and Twelfth Street. The memorial was erected in 1969 to commemorate the most-decorated United States warship in World War II. The memorial contains numerous parts of the battleship that were salvaged when it was scrapped in the early 1960s. Today it is the site of the annual reunion of the sailors and officers who served on Battleship X. Author's photo

Costello Terminal at Joe Foss Field was completed in 1970. It replaced the original terminal building erected by the army during World War II which could no longer handle the increasing volume of air traffic into Sioux Falls. Photo from the N.S.P. Horizons, Sioux Falls in the 70's

American society, the high technology of lasers, computers and telecommunications. Sioux Falls has kept pace with this modern trend in several ways, but perhaps the most important relate to medicine and banking. The first of these has made Sioux Falls a major regional medical and health-care center, and the second is making it a national credit-card center.

Although Sioux Valley and McKennan hospitals have been in the city since the turn of the century (since 1894 and 1911 respectively), recognition of Sioux Falls as a major regional medical center has been fairly recent. Both hospitals undertook expansion projects in the 1940s and again in the late 1950s, but the plan to coordinate expansion and build complementary areas of medical specialization came only in the sixties. In 1965 the two hospitals hired a Minneapolis consultant to study them, the Sioux Falls community, and the surrounding region in order to "formulate an expansion and modernization plan" for the next two decades. (*Argus Leader*, April 18, 1972) The effect of this plan was ultimately to make Sioux Falls a regional medical center possessing most of the high-tech capabilities of any medical center in the country.

The 1965 plan established an integrated construction schedule for the two hospitals that had one building while the other prepared to build. In 1970, when McKennan completed its new four-story nursing wing and two-story recreation unit, Sioux Valley began phase I of its expansion plan, a four-story wheel-shaped nursing tower. Sioux Valley completed phase I, described as "one of the most sophisticated and comprehensive modernization projects of any medical facility in South Dakota...," three years later. (*Argus Leader*, April 18, 1972) The same year McKennan began its new expansion phase which increased its patient capacity, replaced some old facilities and added room for new programs. McKennan finished its construction phase in 1975 when Sioux Valley undertook phase II of its expansion plan.

But more than mortar and bricks were involved in the two hospital's modernization strategy. In the late sixties and especially in the seventies both hospitals added the latest medical technologies. In 1976 McKennan began using lasers to treat eye problems in diabetes patients. The next year Sioux Valley opened its high-risk infant unit. In 1978 the *Argus Leader* announced that "a regional center for open heart surgery and cardiac catheterization is now in operation at Sioux Valley Hospital," and a few months later

it reported that McKennan had begun nuclear cardiology. Other sophisticated medical capabilities, many involving high tech equipment, were also begun.

As the two hospitals added the latest in technology to their operations, the number of highly skilled physicians increased in Sioux Falls. New medical clinics opened their doors and older ones expanded their staffs to the point that new, larger facilities were required. The association of local hospitals with the University of South Dakota Medical School also had an impact by giving them teaching and research programs, hallmarks of leading medical centers.

In February 1981 a new high technology industry opened its doors in Sioux Falls which the *Argus Leader* described as "a new weatherproof business for a state economy that lives and dies on rainfall." The new business was Citibank, the credit card division of Citicorp of New York. It began in rented quarters with only fifty employees, but from the outset it was a high tech operation with three computers and a phone system able to handle three hundred phone calls at a time. Seventeen months later, when Citibank opened its second new building in the new industrial park north of town, it employed eight hundred and its computer and telecommunication technology had multiplied as well. Citibank opened a third building in 1984 to accommodate its growing workforce that then totalled seventeen hundred. Due to Citibank's presence, the Sioux Falls Post Office possesses more sophisticated technology than any other city of its size in the country, and this capability has already and will undoubtedly continue to prompt other mail intense businesses to locate here.

It is the business climate of South Dakota that attracted Citibank to the state, but local facilities and quality of life convinced it to locate in Sioux Falls. The same is true of the First Bank of Houston, Texas, that opened its new national credit card operation in Sioux Falls in October 1984 under the name First City Bank of Sioux Falls. Michael Gatewood, president of First City Bank, told an *Argus Leader* reporter that his bank chose Sioux Falls because it possessed better telecommunications, post office and air services than other cities they considered. The bank also felt that labor in Sioux Falls was more available and productive than elsewhere. The quality of life in a community is determined by the presence of good schools and other public services as well as parks, museums, and other cultural organizations. Business executives from New

The statue of David by Michelangelo is in Fawick Park in downtown Sioux Falls. The statue was given to the city and to Augustana College in 1972 by Thomas Fawick, a Sioux Falls native who made a fortune as an inventor. Fawick later gave the city and the college a copy of Michelangelo's statue of Moses that was placed on the Augustana College Campus. The statue of David generated considerable controversy in the city when it first arrived. Some felt a nude body displayed in public was not only bad taste but would have a bad effect on the community's moral values. The statue was erected but it was placed facing away from traffic and trees were planted to screen it from the street. Author's photo

The EROS Data Center northeast of Sioux Falls was completed in 1974. The Earth Resources Observation Systems facility is designed to receive and interpret information about the earth from orbiting satellites. The Sioux Falls Development Foundation worked hard to secure the EROS facility near the city, and fortunately Sioux Falls had the right attributes to be selected. The site had to be open and free from obstructions that might interfere with the reception of satellite signals, and its location is geographically central to the lower forty-eight states. Joel Strasser photo

167

York, Texas, or elsewhere find Sioux Falls to be a good place to live and do business.

In the twenty-two years since 1965 Sioux Falls has been transformed. Its downtown has been remade from the retailing center of the region into a banking and office district with some specialty shops and restaurants. Its nineteenth and early twentieth-century downtown buildings are largely gone, replaced by new banks, office buildings and parking lots. The focus of retail shopping in the city is now on the major shopping malls along west Forty-first Street. Here is the new "downtown" of the city with its department stores, shops, restaurants, auto dealers and motels. There are other mini-malls around the city, like there were corner groceries in the old days, but Forty-first Street is where serious shopping occurs. The result has been an accelerated development of the south-western part of the city and a consequent need to provide that area with new and improved streets and new schools.

The remaking of Sioux Falls has also been due to the modern technology of computers, telecommunications and space-age medicine. Sioux Falls has become a leading regional medical center because its two major hospitals enlarged their facilities and adopted the latest medical technologies available. But the major impact of computer-age technology upon Sioux Falls has been in the banking and credit card industry. Computers and satellite communications have allowed

Citibank and First City Bank of Sioux Falls to locate national credit card operations in Sioux Falls. And the presence of these two large-employer high-tech businesses is likely to attract others.

The high quality of life also makes Sioux Falls an attractive place to live and to work. Effective city government has provided necessary public services such as good streets, schools, parks, and police and fire protection. The city's quality of life has recently been enhanced by the creation of biketrails, extensive playing fields, and new park areas along the river. In addition, the cultural life of the city, which depended heavily upon the two local colleges prior to 1965, has been broadened and enriched by the creation of the South Dakota Symphony, the Civic Fine Arts Center, the Siouxland Heritage Museums, the Civic Dance Association and the Sioux Falls Community Playhouse.

In the end, however, the essence of any community is its people, and Sioux Falls has always been blessed with men and women who have worked to make their city a better place to live and work. Sioux Falls has been and continues to be a city with a strong booster spirit, for boosters, like those original townsite speculators who came here to build a town by the falls, have known that their own well-being and prosperity are tied to the well-being and prosperity of the community.

This view looks west on Forty-first Street in 1975. The Western Mall is in the foreground and the Empire Mall is nearing completion beyond the river. Forty-first Street had not yet been widened, nor has much commercial development occurred along its route. The malls stimulated a rapid commercial development along Forty-first Street and boomed the residential development of the Western Heights area. Joel Strasser photo

The southeast corner of Ninth and Phillips was photographed in 1974 as preparations were being made to erect the new First National Bank Building. The next building and the bank's old building beyond were both razed after the new bank was completed in 1976. In the background is the Sioux Falls Paint and Glass Company Building that was also removed at this time. First National Bank photo

During the previous decade the parking problem in downtown Sioux Falls had been addressed and this 1975 photo shows several open areas for parking. This was the year the Empire Mall opened and J.C. Penney's closed its downtown store. There was more parking downtown but fewer reasons to go there. Downtown was becoming a banking and office district. Joel Strasser photo

169

This photo shows the Empire Mall from the southwest in 1983. The five-million-dollar shopping complex, like a magnet, had attracted many new businesses to its immediate vicinity by this time: in 1977 La Belle's, in 1979 the Hy Vee and Sunshine Food Markets, and Target, and in 1980 the New Town Mall as well as a number of restaurants, auto dealerships and motels. With easy access and free parking, West Forty-first Street has become the regional shopping center, attracting people from a fifty to one-hundred-mile radius. Empire Mall photo

A portion of the center court of the Empire Mall is pictured here in 1985. Author's photo

This view to the northeast shows the 1987 construction of a new wing at the Empire Mall. This new addition will raise the number of stores to 190 including Sears as the mall's fourth anchor store. Sears, the first major department store to leave downtown, becomes the last to move to the malls when they open at the Empire in the Spring of 1988. Author's photo

170

A rapid increase in the number of college-age young people in the post World War II period and the college's continuing reputation for educational excellence increased Augustana's enrollment from about six hundred students in the 1950s to nearly two thousand students in 1985. The expanded enrollment required the addition of several new buildings during that period including the Morrison Commons in 1960, the Gilbert Science Center in 1965, the tower dormitories in 1969, the Humanities Center in 1971, the library expansion in 1980, and the new chapel in 1982. Augustana College is planning to begin construction of a new physical education and recreation facility in the summer of 1986. Augustana College Archive photo

President William Nelsen (left center), Director of Admissions Dean Schueler, student body president Tom Erickson, and others help launch the orientation program for new Augustana College students in the fall of 1983. Augustana College Archive photo

171

The Sioux Falls College campus was photographed in 1983. This Baptist college has experienced a 300 percent increase in enrollment since the 1950s with a student body of almost nine hundred students in 1985. Major building additions to the campus in the past few decades include three dormitories in the 1960s, the Salsbury Student Union in 1963, the Mears Library in 1965, the Salsbury Science Building in 1967 and the Jeske Fine Arts Center in 1971. Sioux Falls College Archives photo

The Delbridge Museum and entrance to the Great Plains Zoo was completed in 1984. The museum contains the extensive Henry Brockhouse collection of mounted wild animals. Brockhouse, a life-long big game hunter displayed his animal collection at his West Sioux Hardware Store until his death in 1980. C. J. Delbridge, a Sioux Falls attorney, purchased the collection from the Brockhouse estate and gave it to the city on the condition it provide a suitable facility for exhibiting the animals. As a result, this unique collection has been kept intact and in Sioux Falls, and the animals are displayed in their natural-like settings for all to see. Author's photo

The interior of the Delbridge Museum showing a portion of the Brockhouse mounted animal collection. Author's photo

This view looks north from the tower of the Old Court House in 1985. The warehouse district has changed little since the turn of the century with most of the buildings still actively in use. In 1987 this scene was changed by the razing of the Blauvelt Building, lower left, and the Sioux Falls Trolley Barn directly to its south, not pictured. The entire warehouse district, from the Court House to the river has been placed on the National Register of Historic Places. Author's photo

This photo was taken looking southeast from the tower of the old Court House in 1985. Raven Industries in the upper left has occupied the old Manchester Biscuit Buildinng since the company left town in 1960. On the far right is the River Tower Apartment Building constructed in 1972 and in the center is the refurbished Albert House Hotel. Author's photo

Except for the buildings in the immediate foreground, practically all the buildings in this 1985 photo have been constructed since 1965. The two major buildings are the First Bank of South Dakota erected in 1965 and the Holiday Inn built in 1972. The contrast between this 1985 photo taken looking south from the tower of the Old Court House, and a similar one taken in 1905, found in Chapter IV, p. 84, is striking. Author's photo

In the upper left is St. Joseph's Cathedral completed in 1917 and next to it is Cathedral School built in 1926. In the upper center of this 1985 photo is the new Hawthorne School completed in 1985 which incorporates the old Minnehaha Springs Building as an entrance. At the bottom left of the picture is the Minnehaha County Court House completed in 1962 and to its right is the City-County Public Safety Building erected in 1977 to replace the old County Jail and to house the Sioux Falls Police Department. Author's photo

The Court House Plaza, built in 1972, is the home of KSFY TV, which began broadcasting in 1960 as KSOO TV, the second television station in the city. Two other major structures in this 1985 view are the Northwestern Bell Telephone Building in the upper left, erected in 1971, and the Sioux Falls Public Library at the center left, built in 1973. The Civic Fine Arts Center now occupies the old Carnegie Library Building at Tenth and Dakota Avenue. Author's photo

This view is toward the southwest from the Western Bank Building at Ninth and Phillips in 1985. In 1980 the entire east and south sides of Block Eleven (immediate foreground) were razed. A public parking ramp filled the void on the southwest corner of the block, while the new Western Surety Building, on the right, was constructed on the northeast corner. With a bank as the major first floor tenant of the Western Surety Building, the intersection of Ninth and Phillips is surrounded by four banks. Washington High School is the large square building at the upper left of the photo. Author's photo

This view looks toward the southeast from Ninth and Phillips in 1985. Immediately on the right is the First National Bank Building erected in 1975-76. Further up on the right can be seen the Midland Life Insurance Company Building constructed in 1978, and in the center is the Tower of David Apartment Building completed in 1977. Author's photo

This view toward the south from Tenth Street shows Phillips Avenue after the re-opening of the street to traffic. The pedestrian mall installed in 1973-1974 to help save the downtown shopping district, proved to be too little too late, with the end result being the reopening of the block in 1986. Author's photo

This view is toward the east from Ninth and Phillips in 1985. The warehouse and rail yard area on the left has been affected by the reduced rail traffic into the city in recent decades. Along the east bank of the river is the bike trail, a heavily used paved pathway that extends from Falls Park along the river to west Forty-first Street. The trail system was begun in 1977 as part of the city's river development program. Author's photo

Lincoln High School Cross-Country and Track Coach Richard Greeno leads members of his 1987 cross-country team on a strenuous workout along the bike trail. In the nineteen years since coming to Lincoln, Greeno has led his Patriots to eleven State and thirteen Sioux Interstate Conference Cross-Country championships and seven State and fourteen Conference Track championships. Author's photo

The Sioux Falls downtown skyline in 1985 was photographed from the roof of the new Hawthorne School. Dominated by bank and office buildings, the new downtown skyline illustrates the recent development of a white-collar, service-oriented economy in Sioux Falls. Only the Zip Feed Mill at the upper left of the photo reminds us of the agricultural base that remains so important to the city. Author's photo

This photo of Ninth and Minnesota Avenue was taken looking east in 1985. The block in the immediate foreground has perhaps changed least in the past twenty years. The Watkin and Leavitt Garage, built in 1919, is occupied by Kindler Pontiac, Cadillac, the only automobile dealer still downtown. Other buildings on that block and the building directly behind Central Fire Station, also erected by automobile dealers in the late teens, have been converted to other uses. The only change to the exterior of the Central Fire Station is the metal cap that has replaced the handsome old bell tower. Consequently, the city's historic fire bell sits on the ground near the corner. Author's photo

This view, looking east from the Big Sioux River in the Fall of 1987, shows the rapid development along West Forty-ninth Street. This increasingly important artery to the Empire Mall and its surroundings was opened in 1980. In 1982 the street was extended over Interstate 29 from Louise Avenue to carry traffic to the growing Western Heights area whose 1987 population is approaching fifteen thousand people. Author's photo

The major recent addition to this area around Thirty-fourth and Minnesota Avenue is the new grocery store at Thirty-third and Minnesota constructed in 1979. The grocery business in Sioux Falls, long dominated by the Sunshine Food Markets, became keenly competitive in the 1970s with the addition of several new large stores including three Hinky Dinky stores, a new Sunshine store, two Hy Vee stores, a Safeway store, and Albertson's. The competition produced some casualties. Hinky-Dinky closed out its stores in 1984, and three years after opening the largest grocery store in South Dakota at Thirty-third and Minnesota, Safeway discontinued business here. In 1984 Hy Vee purchased the Safeway Building to open its third store in the city. In 1986 Albertson's closed its doors and was replaced by Randall's. Author's photo

McKennan Hospital is shown here in 1985. The several phases of new construction that occurred in the late sixties and seventies transformed McKennan Hospital into a modern facility with up-to-date medical technology and programs, including the first helicopter ambulance service which began operations in May 1986. Author's photo

In the past two decades Sioux Valley Hospital has significantly expanded its nursing capacity and added the latest in medical technology and services. Author's photo

Children play outside the new JFK Elementary School in the fall of 1987. The latest of the new schools built to service the needs of a fast growing population, JFK also helped replace the classroom space lost with the closing of Hayward School in 1986 due to gasoline contamination of the school grounds. Author's photo

The Central Plains Clinic, located at Kiwanis and Thirty-fourth Street, as it looked in 1985. In 1965 the Donahoe Clinic opened at Minnesota and Twenty-fourth Street. Ten years later the new clinic building was already outgrown and a much larger one was constructed here on south Kiwanis. The name was changed to the Central Plains Clinic when the new facility opened in 1976. It currently has fifty-three physicians and five psychologists on its staff. Author's photo

The Crippled Children's Hospital and School at 2501 West Twenty-sixth Street is shown here as it appears in 1985. In the 1930s a group of concerned people began efforts to help the crippled children in the community. The polio epidemic of the late 1940s and early 1950s intensified this concern and in 1952 the current building opened with twenty-four children. The hospital and school, which now houses approximately one hundred children, seeks to provide physically handicapped children the best rehabilitation and education program possible. Author's photo

Kenneth Klein is shown conducting the South Dakota Symphony Orchestra during its 1984-85 season. South Dakota Symphony photo

This 1985 view shows the Citibank Complex (foreground) and the Litton Microwave Oven Plant (top) in the industrial park north of Sioux Falls. Litton came to Sioux Falls in 1977 and Citibank opened its first building in July of 1981. These high technology industries were attracted to South Dakota by its favorable business climate of low taxes and minimal regulation and to Sioux Falls because of its high quality and productive labor force, its well-developed transportation facilities, and the community's quality of life. Joel Strasser photo

Cliff Avenue and Fifty-seventh Street is one of the city's most rapidly growing residential areas of the 1970s and 1980s as the Sioux Falls population has increased to nearly ninety thousand people. Joel Strasser photo

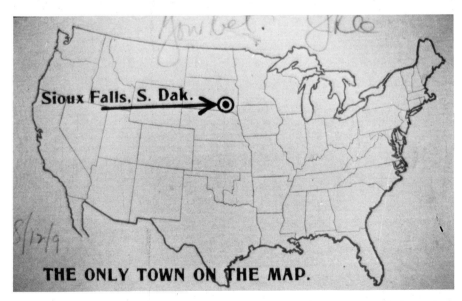

THE ONLY TOWN ON THE MAP.

This shows Southeastern Drive and Forty-ninth Street looking north in 1985. It is only a matter of time before residential growth in this area joins the Hilltop and Tuthill areas together. Joel Strasser photo

A dated postcard from 1909 carries the message that to most Sioux Falls residents is a timeless sentiment. Center for Western Studies photo

The falls of the Big Sioux River are shown here as they appear in 1985. The story of the city began with the falls, and it seems appropriate it should end with them. The falls were admired by early visitors for their beauty and their power. Efforts to tap the falls' power, and the people that crowded into the growing city, soon spoiled the beauty of the area around the falls. At the turn of the century even Seney Island was abandoned to industry and railroads. But in the 1960s some local citizens, and one in particular named Hazel O'Connor, dreamed of restoring the beauty of the falls. Thanks to their efforts, residents and visitors alike can again enjoy the beauty of this special place on the prairie.

On November 7, 1877, the Sioux Falls Pantagraph *published a letter from Miss Carrie J. Peabody of Dubuque, Iowa, who had recently visited Sioux Falls. Her description of her visit included these sentences: "We ford the Sioux, climb a big hill beyond and there lies at a little distance the prettiest of towns, Sioux Falls. We see it through the fading day—too late to visit the 'Niagara of the Northwest,' so we stop at a good hotel for the night." The next morning Miss Peabody visited the falls. "We passed under giant forest trees," she wrote, "crowned with Autumn's kindling glory. Vines were ablaze with scarlet berries, and through the dim arches of the woods came a world of pleasant sounds. Through the foliage we could now and then see the river, where broad, shining leaves of aquatic plants were dreamily floating upon quiet pools. On we go toward the falls . . . soon our eyes catch glimpses of the cascades glittering in the light of the rising sun. There are many water falls, arrested for a moment and then the many cascades finally meet and go laughing, foaming and bounding into the chasm below. . . . From every waterfall and rock Nature with a thousand tongues, proclaims Omnipotence." Author's photo*

Bibliography

Armstrong, Moses K. *The Early Empire Builders of the Great West.* St. Paul, Minnesota: Pioneer Press Company, 1901.

Bailey, Dana R. *History of Minnehaha County, South Dakota.* Sioux Falls: Brown and Saenger, 1899.

Bragstad, R. E., *Sioux Falls in Retrospect.* Privately published, 1967.

Ellerd, Arthur A. *Sioux Falls, The City of Efficient Government, 1909-1916.* Sioux Falls: Mark D. Scott, 1916.

Horton, Arthur G., ed. *An Economic and Social Survey of Sioux Falls, South Dakota, 1938-39.* Privately published, 1939.

Jennewein, J. Leonard and Boorman, Jane, eds. *Dakota Panorama.* Freeman, S. D.: Pine Hill Press, 1961.

Karolevitz, Robert F. *Challenge: The South Dakota Story.* Sioux Falls: Sioux Falls Printing, Inc., 1975.

"Know and Grow with Sioux Falls and South Dakota." *Sioux Falls Journal.* March 8, 1924.

Lekness, Keith, "Electronic Media." *Prairie People.* Vol. I, No. 2, 1978.

Lekness, Keith, "Soldiers in Sioux Falls? That's Right!" *Prairie People.* Vol. 2, No. 1, 1979.

Lekness, Keith, "The Big Sioux River." *Prairie People.* Vol. 1, No. 3, 1978.

McKinney, D. L. and Schlosser, George, eds. *In and About Sioux Falls.* Sioux Falls: Brown and Saenger, 1898.

Olson, Gary D. *Guide to the Microfilm Edition of the Richard F. Pettigrew Papers at the Pettigrew Museum, Sioux Falls, S. D.* Sioux Falls: Center for Western Studies, 1977.

Olson, Gary D. "The Historical Background of Land Settlement in Eastern South Dakota." Arthur R. Huseboe, ed. *Big Sioux Pioneers, Essays About the Settlement of the Dakota Prairie Frontier.* Sioux Falls: Augustana College Press, 1980, 17-28.

Richard F. Pettigrew Papers, Pettigrew Museum, Sioux Falls.

Schell, Herbert S. *History of South Dakota.* Lincoln, Nebraska: University of Nebraska Press, 1968.

Schell, Herbert S. *South Dakota Manufacturing to 1900.* University of South Dakota Business Research Bureau, Bulletin No. 40, 1955.

Sioux Falls Argus-Leader. May 1, 1886 to present.

Sioux Falls Centennial Inc. *The Sioux Falls Centennial (1856-1956) Souvenir Program.* 1956.

Sioux Falls Daily Pantagraph. 1874-1881.

Sioux Falls Daily Press. January 3, 1885-1928.

Sioux Falls Department of Community Development. *Downtown Urban Renewal: Review and Reaction,* 1976.

Sioux Falls Development and Northern States Power Company, *Horizons, Sioux Falls in the '70's.* 1973.

Sioux Falls Industrial Development Foundation and Northern States Power Company, *Sioux Falls, South Dakota.* 1965.

Sioux Falls Public Schools, *A Century of Progress, Sioux Falls Public Schools, 1873-1973.* 1973.

Smith, Charles A. *Minnehaha County History.* Mitchell, S.D.: Educator Supply Company, 1949.

Index

188

About the Authors

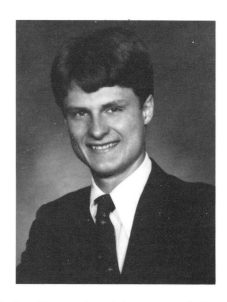

Gary D. Olson, a professional historian by training, has published primarily on topics relating to early American history and specifically on the revolution and confederation periods. He is currently serving as a consultant to Yale University Films in their planning for a film on loyalists in the American Revolution.

But Olson has also applied his research and writing skills to South Dakota and Sioux Falls history since joining the Augustana College faculty in the fall of 1968. In the early 1970s he and a colleague began the photo collection at the Center for Western Studies that currently contains over three thousand slides on Sioux Falls history. In 1974 he joined with Herbert Krause to write *Custer's Prelude to Glory: A Newspaper Accounting of Custer's 1874 Expedition to the Black Hills.* Shortly after that he received a grant from the National Historical Publications and Records Commission to organize and microfilm the Richard F. Pettigrew papers. From 1971 to 1976 he served as Executive Director of the Center for Western Studies, an archival agency, located on the campus of Augustana College, dedicated to the scholarly study of the Upper Prairie Plains Region. He also served as Chair of the Board of Directors of the Siouxland Heritage Museums from 1974 to 1980. Olson has been a frequent speaker to local organizations on Sioux Falls history, and he has presented papers and published articles on topics relating to South Dakota and Sioux Falls history.

Olson received his B.A. degree (Cum Laude) from Luther College, Decorah, Iowa, in 1961, and his M.A. and Ph.D. degrees in history from the University of Nebraska, Lincoln, in 1965 and 1968 respectively. He taught history at Augustana College until his appointment as Dean of Academic Services and Director of Graduate Studies there in 1981. He and his wife Rosaaen are the parents of three sons.

Erik L. Olson, the eldest son of Gary D. and Rosaaen Olson, is currently in his second year of graduate study at Indiana University. He received his B.A. degree from Augustana College in 1983, graduating with Cum Laude honors. His part in preparing this book constituted his summer job in 1985.

Due to the short time frame available to complete the manuscript and his father's busy schedule, Erik's contribution to the project was essential to its accomplishment. Erik brought to the project the research and writing skills he had developed during his liberal arts undergraduate education. He also brought to it a genuine fascination and enthusiasm for the history of Sioux Falls. Erik's interest in local history was stimulated by his research work for the Sioux Falls City Planning Office during the summer of 1982. It was his research that formed the basis for the successful nomination of the McKennan Park area as an historic district on the National Register of Historic Places. That project acquainted him with the places, people and stories that are the essence of Sioux Falls history. It also taught him about where one finds information relating to past events in Sioux Falls. And, as he puts it, the project "hooked" him on architectural history. Given all this, it seems unlikely that this book will be Erik's last involvement with local history.